A FEW THINGS
YOU DIDN'T KNOW

PART TWO

NELLIE ADDISON

authorHOUSE®

AuthorHouse™
1663 Liberty Drive
Bloomington, IN 47403
www.authorhouse.com
Phone: 833-262-8899

Published by AuthorHouse 06/18/2021

ISBN: 978-1-6655-2094-2 (sc)
ISBN: 978-1-6655-2100-0 (e)

Print information available on the last page.

IN THE YEAR OF 2000, Nellie got married to a man name Bobby Addison, he was born and raised in Moscow and Pine Bluff Arkansas, Nellie had knowned him for about one year, they got together after there divorce from there first marriage and moved in a trailer on the same land that her mother who also name Nellie and father Lardeen the man they called Deen lived until there death, and at that time Nellie's sister Liz was slowly but surly geting her house fixed up next door to move back home. Nellie talked to Liz almost every day and she had finally maded up her mind to leave Little Rock where she was staying with her oldest daughter Charlette. But before she came to Pine Bluff and stayed with her baby sister Nellie and her husband Bobby until her house was put in place because her trailer she bought stayed on the side of Fifth Street for a week until the movers could find some body to set her tralier house in place next door to Nellie, they had to use heavy equitment to get her house in the right spot. Meanwhile Nellie and husband Bobby was trying to now enjoy married life, they never took the time for a honeymoon because that particular year there was a ice strom in Arkansas, like never before at least Nellie can't remember one as bad as that one, all untilitys was off for about two weeks and when they got the lights cut back on it was time for Bobby to go back to work because he had refused to leave Nellie alone in the ice strom but it was much pretty ok because he was superviser over housekeeping, he had to make sure that his people that worked under his leadership was there doing the job. Bobby's mother Lenora had passed away in Chicago Ill. Just a year earlier and he was dealing with that great lost plus he was not feeling much better health wise but he stayed in Chicago until his mother passed. Also in a two year time when he was in the army, stationed Germany he had to keep coming back to the USA. To attend his two brothers funerals in Chicago, Sylvester and younger brother Willie, also his grandmother in Arkansas, marry Mcmiller and his three Aunts Maxine, Viloa, and Eveon, all with in two years so he hardly had time to greve and get over one before another family member would pass away and Nellie was having the same problem with so many of her relatives passing away, away, her father, mother, Uncle Henry. All of her uncles in Michigan, and aunts, cousins in St. Louis California and Pine Bluff Arkansas in a very short period of time so like Bobby these deaths was happining so fast she did not have time to get over one before another one passaway, this was so hard on both of them because you could see it on there faces and when they learn about each other siminlar degree of lost love ones back to back they realized that each had more in common than dancing and partying, Nellie started talking to Bobby on the phone and found out that he had gone to the same school name Coleman and did not know each other, and he had gone to a school name Southeast in Pine Bluff. She knew one of his uncles on his daddy's side of the family, every body called him Mut, he was a dark skin good looking man and he married a woman name Helen, she was a very pretty light skin woman with long hair and all the men in the neighborhood was crazy about her, they had two beautiful children a boy and girl they lived down the street from Nellie and she use to baby sit for them, Helen was a run around girl, her step father ran a little place out of his house where you could go get a drink of whisky, sometime pretty girls would hang out there to beat a or some men out of money, others to gamble. Helen was raised up in that house, it was ok while her mother lived but she passed away. Things got worse, her step father had to finish raising her. Helen would go out on Friday and Saturday nights with other men while staying with Mut and her two kids this talk was all around in the neighborhood, heard about it and got very mad because Nellie and the people loved them. Mut was very unhappy because he really loved her, but there's an old saying that go's like this you can't make a house wife out of a street woman. Bobby's daddy Londan Addison passed away in the late ninetys it was a sad time, Bobby has brothers one name Fredie and one Londan Jr.

and one name Clifton, a sister name Linda Faye and one step sister name Bobbie, also a sister name Maple she was the oldest one of the Addison family, she died about three years ago, she use to come around all the time, and her husband whom we called OV, we really missh her laugh, and beautiful personality, all of them live in Arkansas except Fredie, he lives in Floria with his wife Brigit and kids. Nellie dreams of the whole family getting together on a happy occasion, because just last year the family lost there mother Roseie Lee Addison, that was real hard on the Addison family, she died a few years ago, but with the grace of God we have sevived this sorrow once again. Bobby opened a fortune cookie last week and the little paper inside read stop your search, what you are seeking is already yours. Nellie loved this message because everyone she know seem to be searching for the right relationship, the perfect job, the flawless body, we all constantly are looking for more than we already have, and Nellie is quilty as the next person, why do we do this? Her mother would have said we are all cursed with ambition in a way she would have been correct, because most of us are ambitious and we want the best, there's nothing wrong with this of course these seachings should make us better people, sometimes though the treasures we seek are in our grasp and we are blind to that reality, we don't reconize what we allready have. There's a corollary to this, Nellie call it the unexpected treasure this is when we search for one thing and discover another. Nellie in this story is sometime call Frances is searching for legitimacy. She wants once and for all to be someone others look up to, what she doesn't realize that she already has this respect. From all the people that really count any way. And Bobby's looking for a truth that he already know, he's been abled to deny the reality for some time but his eyes are about to be opened in a way he can no longer ignore. Together Nellie and Bobby begain their search, there past interwoven as tightly as a braid, both come to realize the answers they already knew and then they discover somthing better, somthing they weren't even seeking in the first place. They encounter the unexpected treasure, in all your search, Nellie hope you find the same success, just remember be open to unepected treasures and consider the idea that what ever you are seeking it might allready be yours. Nellie went through hell a living hell on earth, trying to make their marriage be loveing, happy, and peaceful, but it was no walk in the park, or lovely happy evening dinners or what ever. It was hell, it was nothing like she was accustom to. Bobby got a job at the small town only hospital, working yard service from temporary unemployment agency, we discussed this job and prayed over it and come to the conclution that he needed to work his way up to a inside job for more money, more than Nellie's little disabilitys SSI checks, which was about at that time four hundred fifty eight dollars a month, and

Bobby was getting two hundred fifty five dallors every two weeks so between the both of them they were bringing in about nine hundred sixty eight dollars a month and about fifty dollars worth of food stamps, but also they were paying four hundred dallors a month on the trailer, but at least they were buying it, utility bills meant keeping the lights off useing less electricity as possible not being abled to buy nice cloths or shoes, but some how they knew that God was going to make a way, they could not see a way out of this, but God could, VA. approved Bobby for fifty percent disability at that time so he got a lump sum of money that got them out of debt and a nice little check a month which was a big help and that money had to be managed very carefully. Then Bobby and Nellie started argueing about Bobby being to friendly with other women and all Nellie did was stay at home cleaning, washing, and swepining water out the back door, because the washing machine was no good, Nellie had purchased it from a little junk yard across the street from a fast food place for fifty dollars and it worked ok for a little while but after a few month when it spin it would shake the whole trailer and was so loud, Nellie did her washing before dark because Bobby was at work trying to get placed from yard work to inside of the hospital as superviser over house keeping and he did, but things were so bad mentally and physically for Nellie, she was suffering and it seem like nobody nobody cared about her feelings, just only what they could get out of her, money mostly, they must have thought that sence she had a new house and car that she was all right, she had to figure out how to pay all their bills and get them off every month, keep food on the table, keep from arguring about stupit things. With so little money that was coming in there home at that time. Oh Nellie was proud of Bobby for being promoted as superviser over house keeping, but he seem to all ways put her in second place, he had more money and things should have gotten better may be it did they would go to the movies or some other recuration, a Nellie had applyed for two credit cards, she was approved and went right on to sears and got a brand new washer and dryer, a slow cooker, and some nice dress suits to wear to the kingdom hall, Bobby got him some really nice dress suits to wear to the hall, and shoes and he also got a new living room set, the sofa was a big fluffy sectional, it fitted in a wide circle all the way around the room and two gold glass end tables and a coffee table just the same a as the two end tables, it was so pretty in that trialer, so cozy a and comfortable, Bobby went to work at three pm to eleven pm from Monday through Friday, then he started working on Saturdays to make over time money. Nellie thought like he's all ready gotten a raise why do we need extra money? Now that we are up on our feet, then one day before he got ready to go to work Nellie was looking for some business papers and he told her to look in the back seat of car, she saw some avon perfume in a avon bag, so Nellie went back in the house and confronted Bobby about this perfume in the back floor of the car and he came up with this dumb excuse about some woman that he worked with asked him if she could put this package in his car until she get off of work, right then and there Nellie Bobby knew they needed each other more than any other man or woman would be able to do for them, but Nellie wanted to break up because there were to many signs of Bobby being unfaithful and the hurtful things he would say, and he knew that Nellie was a Christian and she had to go by the bible, what it said, and Nellie felt like he was useing this and she was hurting and Bobby was being very incensity to her feelings, or was it one of satans tricks, because she had been married before, when she was a younger woman, she was about ninteen years old when she got married to her first husband Andre Harris and he was only twenty one years old, so they were to young to completly understand the game of the world or the patients, it took to be a child of God at this point, and there was a lot of people aganist them in Pine Bluff Arkansas there home town, because of the murder that took place at Coleman High School, but they had the wrong bush girl it was Lillian Busch no relation, there was a lot of rumors going around in town that Nellie was connected which was a lie put out by Lillian Busch family and friends or someone who really hate Nellie because the lies keep going for years after. Andre Nellie's first husband had testifyed at a drug dealer trial and they used his testimony to put this drug dealer in prison, so he only told the truth and freed his friends from going to prison, for something that was not his or their doing, they were at a set or party where there was all kinds of drugs and the police was watching this particular dealer and the ones there was arrested and was going down with the guiltyones but they knew that they was not dealing no drugs from this man under arrest so they told the truth on him, and they were release, after that Andre allways thought someone was watching him, and this rumor going around town about Nellie being involed in the murder at Coleman High School, was a lot of pressure on both of them so Nellile decided to move, and decided out of the state of Arkansas Andre agreed and they moved to Memphis Tennessee, because they did not want to leave at all but they had to. ALL of their family was in that little town, and they didn't want to go to fare from there parents, and other family they were just big kids both caught in a trap and needed some relief. Every thing was going so fast and she did not want to expose other family members to the trouble they were going throught at that time, it was real hard in Memphis, they had to depend on Andres mother Marian Harris a little to much, she helped them with rent and utility bills for a short time until Andre got a job at this rubber comany and Nellie got a job at this hospital right down the street from where they stayed on Wakins Street she was making only one hundred twenty five every two weeks it don't sound like much but back then the minumum wage was a lot less than now, and she never did find out what Andre weekly sallary was because it ranged differant from week to week, it was so hard but they got enough to pay the bills to sevive, and they went out to eat, movies, and any where they wanted to for fun. Then Nellie found out that Andre had not been paying the rent. So they had to move from a place she loved, and knew her way around. Andre said don't worry I got this and with in two days they was moving out of that nice apartment where Nellie could walk out on her private terrance or balcony and watch the cars and people on the streets, with the wind blowing in her face, it felt so good, Nellie could walk any where she wanted to in that little area it was a good area at that time, she did not want to move up in that part of the city, it was a nice apartment but she did not know her way around, but she caught on fast by that time Nellie was missing her home so she called and her brother Bob told her that something was wrong with her neice Ethal, Nellie asked him what? He said talk to mom she got the phone, it was so good hereing her mother's voice when she told Nellie that Ethal had broken up with Robert Clark Ethal's boy friend at that time, they was allready smokeing pot, then Ethel started going out to night clubs which she did not normally do with out Nellie or some other family member or friend, and to Nellie that could only mean trouble so Nellie call called Ethel mother's house and asked her would she like to come to Memphis for a little while until she get better and she said yes because Nellie thought that there was no other way. They both needed each other, yes the two girls needed each others help. So Nellie and Andre sent for her and then Andre called his mother Marian and asked her to pick Ethel up and take her to the bus station in Pine Bluff and put her on the bus headed to Memphis, Nellie and Andre picked her up brought her home with them that Sunday evening and got her settled in. That Monday Andre went to work, the phone was not connected yet, so Nellie and Ethel walked down about two blocks to a real beautiful apartment where Nellie really wanted to stay, and used the phone in the lobby, she left then Nellie told her mom that Ethel had made it to Memphis ok, her mom whom Nellie was named after, she told Nellie that Ethel was having some nerve problems like her, before she lift, mom said hope that this trip would help her and make sure that they both get some rest and be good to each other they did not rest much because at that time Memphis was a faster town than Pine Bluff Arkansas, but they were good to each other and they partyed together, smoked weed, and Andre interduced her to a tall dark man name Larry, he worked at the same place Andre work, he was real kind and nice young man that seemed to like Ethel a lot so they exchanged phone numbers. Then it was time for Ethel to go home, she seemed a lot better and Nellie was happy and sad because Ethel was leaving and happy because she was better and could go home and start a new life. After that Nellie and Andre left Memphis and traveled all over the country of the beautiful USA. To places like Chicago, Detrot, St. Louis, New York, Los Angeles, Compton, Bearcly, Oaklnd and Nellie finally worked her back to Arkansas, they moved to Fort Smith Arkansas, where her husband was born and raised in the same house, it was a really big house but they could not seem to get it fixed up like they wanted to, but they stayed in there a long time where Nellie lost five babys, after the last baby died which almost took her life, she healed, she left Fort Smith, went back home to Pine Bluff Ark. Where Nellie thought she could rest and get over such a great lost, it was at first but in just a little while the house came following down on her literaly, Nellie had fixed up her parants house as well as she could by buying paint and rugs and tile for the kitchen floor, the other floors did not need any as bad as the kitchen, they low and behole the house started to fall down on her, starting with her mothers sealing caveing in not all the way just kind of hanging there for all to see and she did not have the money to get this fixed for her mother. This hurt her to the soul, and she thought about some thing that she had read in the bible about you should not sading the Holy

Spirit which was there because she prayed for it to come, and help her because she did not know how to do the things she was doing, it had to be the Holy Sprit of God, and that is one of the things the bible says God will not forgive you for. She can't began to tell you how deep cuting to her soul this pain in her heart, and she allready was hurt to the core over loseing her five babys, husband, she felt like her life was over, and the shame of the cealing there for all to see and judge the Bush family, but let me tell you something this family survived because Nellie's three brothers at that time, Robert, LB, and Floyd Bush pulled together and got some men they knew, the head man was Lorde Lyon he and a couple of who he could get that day every day different men worked in that house for months until they got it livable right next door to momys old house that her husband Deen build her house. She moved in her new house, it was not a manion but it sure was a lot better than that old house which was following in on us. Nellie come from a poor family and she's not ashamed of that because it keeps her humble and understanding to all those people trying to get over in this world of turn up noses and people looking down on poor folks, she don't care how fore she go in this world, even if you are ontop of the world. What good is it for a man to gain the whole world and lose his soul? don't mean that you should not want a better life for you and family, but don't get to the point where you can't feel for your faller man who have not made it to the point where you are, help each other! This is the key to happyness for man kind. Stop hateing each other, for one, not having as much as you, or may not be as educated as you are. Remember that old time common sense is what this country started off with. The bible is like a letter God telling every body what to do and what not too do until he fix things to be safe and happy again. Look it up in your bible if you don't have one I suggest you go get one, in other words look out for your after life as well as right now. When and first came home, Rodney and Clifton Jr. was still staying with her parents, Rodney was in the eleven grade at Watson Chapel High School, and Clifton was in the ninth or tent grade at Watson Chapel High, his father Clifton Sr. had met a woman name Jackey, she and Dume whom we called Clifton Sr. hooked up, she lived on the east side of town, with her mother and baby sister, she and Dume had falloned in love at that time and every thing was going ok for them. They seemed to be happy, because Nellie use to go over to Dume's house at least twice a week and Jackey would be at his house, she had three kids which Dume liked a lot, Nellie can remember before Christmas one year Dume had her and Bobby help him get three bikes from the pawn shop not fore from his house for the kids, it was so funny because Bobby and Dume could not get the bikes in Nellie's car, so he and Bobby had to ride the two bikes to Dume's house, they went the back road,

Nellie was following them slowly, in her car and Willie Compton was coming down the same street and he stoped his car and started laughing because Dume and Bobby was very tall men and there legs was sticking out on the side of those bikes like the clowns in the parades, that day they made so many people laugh out loud, but they got the bikes back to Dume's house before the kids got out of school and had time to hide them.

Nellie can also remember Dume and Jackey and her consin Rita, Liz, Robert, Floyd and Lardeen Jr (LB) and others, they would go to there little get togethers and there was good food and drinks and good conversation. The family had found out that Dume was ill, and he was not going to get any better without a bone merrow tranplant and Nellie and the rest of the family all had to go to the doctor and take a test to find out which one of them matched better with Dume's blood type all except LB, because he said that he was to sick and old, Robert, Elizabeth, Floyd and Nellie went to the doctor to take the test that might just save our brother Dume's life. Every body matched up about 75% and Nellie matched up 90% Nellie was suppose to have a operation to take some bone merrow out of her to transplant into Dume's body to fight off the kind of cancer he had, and Nellie waited for weeks to do this and the doctor did not call her and she decided to ask Jackey had she heard from the doctor about the operation and she said no, Nellie begain to get worried because they needed to do this before Dume go into crisis then there would be no hope at all for Dume to live. So Nellie went over to Dume's house to talk to him and he said that's all right sis don't worry about it I have decided not to take the operation after all, Nellie said Dume I will do this you know this, Dume said I don't want you to lose your life tring to save me and they argued, but Nellie could not change his mine, it was made up so that was that. Dume and Jackey had been ingagede for a while and they got married at Jackey's mothers house one Saturday afternoon, it was a beautiful wedding. They all went over to Dume's brothers house Robert to salarbrate. Earlier that year Dume had put in a lawsuit in against the company he worked for and where he got hurt, Nellie asked Dume what happen and he told her that he picked up a can that must have had something left inside and as he picked the can up it sprayed him all in his chest and a few nonths later he was diagnosed with cancer. Dume and Jackey got chance to be married and together for a short period of time before he went into crises, Jackey rushed him to the hospital in Pine Bluff, they did what they could for him, then sent him to Little Rock, to Baptist Hospital where there were suppose to be better doctors but it was to late, because they had wasted to much time, they should have contacted Jackey or Nellie before he went into crises, he was up talking when they put him in Baptist Hospital, then the next day Nellie and Liz, dentis her husband, and

Bobby went back to the hospital, the doctors had put tubes in his mouth and he could not talk to them and only a little while he had sliped into a coma. Dume last a week in the Baptist Hospital, that was the worse time or week for Nellie and she assume the rest of the family, she felt so sad, depressed, lonely, and she had thought she was going to lose her mine, she felt like God had abandon her, she had no one to talk to, she had to keep all these feeling inside. She could not find a friend any where that is why she really can not trust any friends, because when she needed them they were no where around, but maybe she had picked the wrong friends, she don't really know, or maybe they did not know what she was going through. Even relatives did not understand, we all are imperfect so our mines might be wrong from time to time, so she asked God to help her to see more deeper to see what other people are going through, this may be the reason they are acting in such a way and the people that can't seem to handal there own problems should not be so rude, and afenceive to others, we have to live together in a civilized society. Don't judge them, God is the judge of all things and he has the last words. The sound of the phone made Nellie come back to the present, and reality and she notice needed to take her corn bread out of the oven. The next day Nellie and Bobby went to the super market, she noticed that at least three woman came up and hugged Bobby, Nellie ask him who was that and he snaped her up saying they are class mates of mine, just a friend, Nellie thought well hell why you got to snap me up, because I ask you a question, she had a right to know who those bad ass woman were disrespecting her like this. Well when he and Nellie started going together it was no woman running up to him because he didn't have a dame thing, as soon as he got this superviser job it was woman comeing from everywhere all up in his face, Nellie and Bobby would fight about that, she told him to get these women straight and to stop disrespecting her or she would, because she was tired and, what kind of fool fool did he think she was this woman Nellie had been all around the world, taught by the best, saw all kinds of games that people play on each other, and she was tired of running from town to town and had decided to stay home in Pine Bluff Ark. And try to fix her life and have a place she could call home. At first she was going back to Calafornia when her mother passed away. She thought what do I have to lose, then Bobby talked her in to staying for a while to see how things work out between the two of them, and it didn't take much talking because her only sister was still alive and her four brothers was alive, her oldest brother. Alfored was still in New York but earllee was in Pinc Bluff in a nurseing home with both of his legs cut off, he loved to go walking so this was very sad to him and his family. His daughter Ethel told Nellie that her brother Standley had put earl in a apartment for old people stayed where they could get proper medical help and there lunch and dinner would be perpared for them. Nellie had heard about apartments kinda like that but Nellie's sprit told her that he was or could be in a nurseing home, the family had growned so fore apart until there was hardly any communication, and mostly every thing was mostly the wrong hear say from running into a relative in a fast food place or grocery store. Earl was a diabetic, he inherited it from his mother. Nellie ended up on Fifth Street with Bobby and both of them was trying to make a big comeback from so much pain and sorrow, Nellie kind of hated winter then she loved it to. Grey days and even darker nights depressed her, with all the extra stress she been under, she let the weather bother her even more, thoughts of home had sliped, in before she could stop them, she'd gotten lost in the past, thinking of things best left alone, with doged determination, she reined in her thoughts, now was not the time to allow her history to haunt her if anything it was more important than ever that she stay firmly in the present. Marian Harris and her son Andre Harris was Nellie's supporters, and they were one of the reasons Nellie had become a writer, years ago before Marian and her son Andre had literally saved Nellie's life, one night Nellie could not sleep so she decided to practice writering, in a book where she was keeping notes of her life experance, Marian tapped the door frame with her finger nails, you aren't getting discouraged are you? Nellie had learned a long time ago that wanting and geting were two very different things, but she said the process does seem to be taking a long time that has noting to do with you my dear, these things simply require a lot of finesse, and that's what you've got. Nellie should have stared back on her paperwork, but instead she turned back to the gloomy window, nothing was for sure there were no guarantees, that was another lesson she learned early in life, a telephone rang down the hall and someone laughed loudly, the sound pulled Nellie a way from her thoughts and made her reallise she needed to get back to work, with much love and gratitude to the late music and English teacher who first inspired Nellie with these words have you ever thought about becomeing a writter? Was Mrs. Marian Harris because it seem to me that you have missed your calling she touched Nellie's life with love of the language, her laughter, and dedication to children with challenges, to live up to the best in themselves. May children allways find there own Marian Harris because it seem like somebody cares. And also to Nellie's mother Mrs. Nellie Jinkins bush who inspired Nellie to love all people, and God's creatures, and to go after what she want, without putting someone that's competition down to build herself up, kids listen to your parents because they have been where you are trying to go and they know more than you think. Nellie started looking out at the gloomy clouds again and remembering when she did not listen to her father, father about a certain boy, and when she did not listen to her father how bad things were, trying to love him when he was so out of control. He only wanted to be so cool among his friends, to be knowned as a player and every one of his friends wanted to be with Nellie, because they would call her talking about going out with them, she told him but the fool never believed her, she thought maybe he knew about it and was testing her. So she call her crazy self being true to him but she was so young and inexperanced, oh! Why didn't she listen to her daddy, so the door was never closed for a long time it made her life hell, just like her daddy said, it took five minutes to get into and thirty years to get of, so kids please listen to your parents. An alarm went off it was Nellie's tea pot sounding like that and she stoped looking out the window on that gloomy day thinking about the past until the next time, so she made her tea and dranked it with some oreo cookies, she watched general hospital and when it went off she put some cloths in the dryer and watched half of Doctor Oz read her bible for her next bible lesson, and she started to look out of the window again, she could not stop herself from thinking about the past, this time it was about her neice Annettee and Earl Lee Jr. Where could he be, he never contact our family, let's say me, how built and handsome he was like his father. Nellie's brother Earl, she don't think he came to his daddy's funeral. She don't think he came to his grandmother's funeral, he may not have knowned they had passed away, sometime she wonder is he dead or alive, sometime people think that nobody, certain ones or no one cares about them, and there are so many they leave behind that truly care about them, and miss them very much. Annette seem to have changed sence she got back from New York, Nellie never see her any more but she got chance to talk to her last week and she is doing (ok) and they are going to get together soon, Nellie can't stop now because she have to finish this project she started back in 2017, maybe she will pause for a while to gather as many relatives and true friends to party one weekend soon as the whether warm up some. Nellie went on to remember how it use to be when her only sister Liz kids were small, Etta, and Caroline stayed with there grandmother, Nellie's mother's house is where all of them use to stay, Liz would bath them every morning wether they were going to school or not, she combed there hair which Liz would put there hair up in those same three poney tail, all the time with little ribons or clamps on the tail, the girls did not complan much because they knew that there poor grandmama, mother, and Aunt Nellie was doing the best they could under the bad circumstance. One day Nellie and Liz found out that there cooking stove had stopped working and they had to use a two eye hot plate to do all there cooking on, it was ok in the summer time but when it got cold, Liz and Nellie was trying to find an electrical cooking stove and a man that Liz and Nellie knew whom every body called Buddy told Liz about a friend of his, every body called Jucke was suppose to have a electrical cooking stove that he was trying to sale, now Nellie should known better, not to buy something from a man name Jucke for only twenty five dallors, but Nellie needed that stove so badly, because it was really geting cold. There Uncle Henry had come down from staying with his wifes neice Mattie in Little Rock was about sixty miles from Pine Bluff, and big Nellie and Uncle Henry was friends, and in there late seventys and they were not able to do much so she basicly stayed at home with her and Uncle Henry was Deen was big Nellie's husband brother, he did not know that his brother Deen was dead. Nellie had not finished Beaty College yet, her mother took sick and Nellie had to take her to the hospital in Pine Bluff, then they sent her home and she got worse, Nellie took her to Doctor Martha Flowers and she set up an appointment with a doctor in Little Rock Ark. And Robert took them to that app. And the doctor said he was going on vacation, but he was not going to let mother go home vomiting like she was and he signed her in the hospital in Little Rock, Nellie started to take her home until the doctor came back from his vacation but thought that he might be right, because he was a black because he was a black doctor and seemed to care, but black don't mean nothing like it use to, only if you are in the click. My mother stayed in that hospital three days and three and a half nights, Nellie told them that she was a dibetic when they questioned her and the amount of shots she had to take a day. Nellie was staying in the same room with her because she ordered a cort to sleep on because her mother did not want to be left along, Nelli was ill herselft and had left Uncle Henry at home alone, mama said for us to take care of Uncle Henry, and Nellie did her best, with all of the personnal problems she had on her son, everybody did back then the way things were with all of the family, being in shock of so much death in the family, as Nellie was looking on into the yard at the birds and all of the little creatures moving about and she remembered that she did not see the nurse ever come in and give her mother a shot for her diabetes. She had stoped vomiting so they said she could go home Friday and that was Wednesday: so Nellie had been there with her mother every since Monday and that Thursday Liz, Laura, Ethel and Floyd, came to visit, Nellie was so glade because she was going to get them to take her to KFC, and get her a large chicken dinner and to get her some beer, to hide in the room and drink to come her nerves, she can remember being so very tired and depressed, but her mother was coming home the next day which was Friday, made things all better, it was to good to be true. Nellie asked Floyd and Laura to take her to the store to get her dinner but she notice that Floyd was a little reluctant to leave mom alone so sister is who we call

Liz said she would stay until we got back but Floyd was still reluctant and Nellie said to herself maybe I will just wait, but her lust for food and beer made her continue to ask Floyd to take her, and he did and when they got back, as they were going down the hall to there mother's room is when they noticed a lot of nursese and doctors in the hall way telling them to stay back, you could see through the glass windows that they were working on mother, there sister Liz was standing there by the door way becking for them to come fast! That something bad had happened to mom. In just that little time, it only took thirty minutes because we were keeping up with the time this was unbelevable, Nellie and Floyd was devastated beyound repair, after a while they took them in a room, told them that someone would be in shortly to talk to them, and they waited about fifteen minutes then a man came into the room and said that he was sorry but there mother was gone and that they had done all they could, but could not save her, Nellie was so confused because they had told her earlier that her mother was going home the next day, how did this happen? Nellie throw herself on the floor and stared crying like a young child throwing a tandrun, her baby brother Floyd told her to get up or he was going to leave her there so she got up full of all this pain, that she could hardly bear. The only thing helped Nellie was her mother saw her finish cosmetology college with all A's. She finished in nineteen eighty seven and she had an opportunity to open up her own beauty shop, because her sisters husband at that time offered Nellie a chance by opening up a little hamburger stand he had next door to his club. She could turn it into a beauty shop, Mr. Edward Moore was his name but every body called him Ed, Nellie think about those times offten, when Liz and her kids use to ride in that truck he had they seemed to be so happy, it made her feel happy just seeing them happy for the first time. He told Nellie that she could turn it into a beauty shop when ever she wanted to, but that day never came because she did not have the money to fix it up, how was she going to get all of the chimicals, right chairs and shampoo bowls. It has allways been hard times for Nellie it seem like a dark cloud was over her head following her around, she worked so very hard, extra hard and nothing happen (no progress). She learned from studying the bible that when you are doing God's will and working hard and there's no progress then then it just might be a deman and he's some how attached himself to you, this was horrowfying to her when she first found this out, from a man name John Mcintosh and his wife Ruby they use to study the bible with Nellie and her husband Bobby in there home, she use to learn so many things from the bible when John was living he passed away about two years ago. Now Nellie and her husband feel like they are on there own without any assistances and friendship, because John and his wife Ruby felt like family and real friends.

John was an elder praying for her and she really miss those prayers, he is truly missed. Nellie is the type of woman that want's to have her own money, her own every thing, not beholdin to anyone but God. Nellie decided to get a job in a beauty shop, for more training then maybe she could save up the money to open up her own shop, but Nellie found out that people will talk about you and put you down because you may be new and they finished beauty college and been out there for a while think you may not know as must as they do, Nellie thought that they was going to help her, since she was fresh out of school and they hired her to work in there shop and not put them down in front of the customers. It was hard when she decided to stop working to give up fixing hair. But a lot of young girls completly gave up. You know Nellie from her first book call a few things you didn't know, she said we need to remember not to give up, because through all the pain, the hard work, and the mourning of our loved ones, we will rise above it all. We truly can change our life's outcome and destiny if we fight hard for it, a knot on the door, Nellie stoped remembering and answered her door it was her great neice by Liz oldest daughter Challete, and her little girl was standing there so brave and so sweet, Nellie said come in sweetheart! Out of this cold, Nellie was so happy to see her because she was so lonely and sick she had come home to die because Nellie felt that it was her time with all the suffering and sickness she was going through at that time. The little girl name is Tylesa, help Nellie wash her dises and pans, pots and Nellie washed her coat, and gave her some warm soup, she would get off of the bus at Lee Street and walk a block down and turn left on Fifth Street and walk another block down to her Aunt Nellie's trialer where her grandmother and her mother, and her two Aunts Charlotta and Caroline grow up. There house burn down a few years before. The little girl Tylesa wou come allmost every day but her Mama Charlette and Daddy Sylvester Brooks would have to pick her up every evening, and sometime her step father had to pick her up his name is Lemont/Johnson, this was a little to much for them because they worked, and was very tied when they got off of work, so Nellie understood that they was not trying to keep her away from her house. Tylesa mother Charlette told her to get off the bus at her own house and not to get off at Aunt Nellies street, Tylesha got off the bus at Aunt Nellie's house two more times and her mother had to take a more firmer hand withe her, then the visits stoped, and Nellie would be looking for her and she remember that Tylesa wasn't coming anymore, or any of the kids. This was a hard time for Nellie because she was very lonely and sick, Nellie's old friend Sally Ento who she grew up with, lived on Lee Street where she was raised with her two sisters Perl, and Katie, one brother Isaiah and there mother Miss Ethel and Mr. Booker Ento. Was good friends to Nellie's family.

Salt of the earth good people, when there was another friend name Forestine. Sally made friends with her real fast just like Nellie did because she was such a friendly nice girl. We all went to the same school together and really cared about each other. But Nellie started hanging with the wrong crowd. And going to all the wrong places. She started smokeing, cigarettes and drinking. And this was allmost everyday, specially on the weekends. That type of life did not bring her happiness, but it was better than staying at home, looking at the four wall. It seem like they were closing in on her. She was so miserable. She couldn't go to school, couldn't rest or relax at home. It seem like Nellie was under some kind of spell. Nellie had been away from home for a very long time. And moved back in the neighborhood in 1996, she had been gone every since 1974, she also got married, but her marriage did not work out like Sally's did not. Nellie was back home again and it really felt good, everybody was living compared to now, because it seemed like the whole neighborhood is dead now. There's just a hand full of people left. Sally had three children by her husband James Wilberly. Before they broke up. When Sally first saw James, Nellie think that she fell inlove with him, we walking from the corner store and he said wait up and interduced himself, Nellie said are you the one that use to go with Lillian Richards and he said yes how did you know? This is a small to wnand I get around and here things, beside she was a pretty popular girl. That kind of broke the ice for Sally to start talkin to him. Then we got to my house and Nellie said I'll see you later, James walked Sally home, they exchanged phone number's and started dateing. And the rest is history. They got married. Nellie got married and lift town. When she return after fifteen years. They had broken up and Sally started dateing again and had two more girls. All girls grew up to be very pretty independent young ladys with children of there own, before Sally died she came to Nellie's house one day with tear's in her eyes where they grew up playing around there and having fun, they would study the bible sometimes and just talk about everything just like Nellie and Liz did, it was like being around relatives, but that particular day was differint, she asked Nellie to do somthing for her, if she didn't make it to take care of her girls, she went on to explain that she ment if Nellie see them out doing somthing wrong, Sally ment in a way that she did not raise them to behave and Nellie told her that she was going to live long enough to raise her own kids and she did. Nellie sister Liz baby girl Caroline little girl name Courtney started coming every day to see about her until Nellie's sister Liz which was Courtneys grandmother, finally moved next door, boy was Nellie glade that she had come home, she stayed with Nellie for a long time until Liz got the money together which all ways confused Nellie until today is why Liz did not have the money fight then, it finally came to her the reason she did not have the money is because she had given her kids, which is perfectly understanable because most people will help there children, and she loved her kids more than anything on earth, but friends and others who pertend to like her and got over on her good side, she had been down for so long and when she got some money, well most people party and that money can go like wild fire but Liz managed to put a down payment on a brand new trailer house. Liz had put eight thousand dollars down on this new house, at the same place Nellie get hers from, and the same agent that helped Nellie helped Liz and Nellie remembering the man name was Marty, and he told Nellie and Bobby, don't yall let Miss Liz spend all that money up, Nellie could only talk to Liz about it but she would not listen, because she was told that she was going to die, by some doctor but she didn't tell Nellie how long she had or any thing eles, that's the kind of person she was, she had a lot of secrets that's the way Nellie's whole family is maybe they think that she can't handle certain things. So there was no reason to continue asking her because she was not going to get an answer. Then Liz went back and got that eight thousand dollars from Marty. About six months later our friend Marty had a heart attack, Marty was in worse shape then Nellie thought, she went in to pay on her bill for the trailer, she didn't see Marty and asked his wife about him and she told Nellie that Marty had died from another heart attack about a week ago, this news really messed her day up because she knew him from the old neighborhood, Marty knew a loto of people out there in the loop, like Ed Moore, he own a club and store, Earestine and Lue who was simply called Lues. So when his wife told Nellie that he was dead she felt a real bad sadness come over her and that whole day she was sad because Nellie kept on thinking about Marty and how nice he was to her and gave her and husband Bobby a good deal on there trailer, nobody ever gave Nellie a chance, some people allway try to make it hard for a woman put you down and make you look stupit, and keep you under them to build themselves up by puting some one eles down and makeing jokes, laughing and really they are to afraid to persue there own dreams or they are stuck in a real boring job or life not going anywhere and make do with what they have, and people like that are jealous of people that's are doing something with there life, and not runing the streets like a chicken with his head cut off. The world is full of people like that. So after Nellie maded back home she had such a hard time until she offten wished that she had not come home, but her parents were still living and wild horses coulded keep her away, no matter what she had to go through it was worth it just to be near her family, her family had changed so much until she sometime wished she was dead, but she had good news of the kingdom of God was near and what they had to do to get in, at first everybody thought she was crazy and she felt crazy and trying to deliver this message, and the first time around she failed miserably, but Nellie was on a mission to get it right and not to be misinterpret, and found out that its not what you have what in meteral things but when somebody truly love you unconditionaly, without game or tricks to have you under there control and run your life. God do not use tricks and games to control his creation. Because he wants you to love, understand and see his goodness, fairness to all people to make there own decisions, based on the truth about him, because he has not nothing to hide. He want you to love and come to him on your own, free will, he did not create some kind of robots, we all were created with free will, these things he tell you to and not to do is the law his, we are suppose to be doing any way, its for our own good to keep us safe from satans traps that could cost our life to be hard or have harder times while we are on earth in this system of things, because our happyness and long life depends on our decisions and choices we make. Liz third husband brother whom every body called June his wife Iren, neice Alberta, Carolyne, had opened a club on the west side of town and was doing well, they stayed over to that club trying to make a success out of it, Liz had to be spining money cost Nellie know that she did not loan her any money and when she did Nellie paid her back because at one time Nellie and her husband was sleeping on the floor on an box springs and mattress, in a one bedroom apartment on the east side of town. Nellie and Bobby had been planing to get a trailer and put it on some land Nellie's parents had lift to her on the west side near the loop, she wanted to be near her brother and sister her only sister Liz, Floyd, (brother) and Robert, (brother) Bobby was geting ready to move but all those plans were canceled, because Bobby's ex wife took his income taxes for the two boys he had by her and Nellie put there plans on hold until the next year. Then Bobby was free to move over on Fifth Street so Nellie could be near her big sister. But things did not work, the way Liz and Nellie plained it. Nellie only wanted to get out of those apartments because it was to much noise and to many strage people. She wanted to be somewhere around familiar folds, and a group of related individuals. Two sisters planed to grow old and raise there children together, well so much for that dream, because the people, the devil, was not going for that all those heads together. Well so much for that, she jumped for the chance to move on Fifth Street near family and friends she grow up with, and Bobby didn't have any land they could use so they decided to go for it and just have to pay for the trailer and they did. While they were at those apartments, Nellie decided that they needed to make more money to get a bed and get up off that floor, so she come up with the deal to throw newspaper for the city of Pine Bluff, Ark. The next day she set ups a an appointment with the Pine Bluff commercial and they gave them a route, and took her and Bobby around to show them what neighborhood to thow the papers, it was out by the hospital where Bobby worked, but the first night they did not know wheree they was until Bobby saw the profestional building and said Nellie what's wrong with us? Then Nellie could see where they was. They was so nerves and full of fear because every thing looked so foreign at night, Bobby got off work at eleven pm and he and Nellie would go over to the paper company and pick up there papers then go thow them they made a game out of it by seeing which one of them would first miss a drive way Nellie would win most of the time but she had the advantage because he was driveing, they did this for one year, and got a brand new bedroom set after that they filled out the income taxpapers. And waited, soon as that tax money come back they could hardly keep there cool, Nellie started packing immediately, she was thinking this is my only sister and her kids and grand kids. Oh! how Nellie loved them just like her own kids, but somebody messed with there mines, and when it come to her it don't take talk about her to make people to have hard feelings against Nellie. They was Nellie's life and she could not talk or tell any one what she was feeling, she had to bear it all by herself. Nellie taught Liz little girls, Carletta, and Caroline because Liz oldest girl was staying with her daddy's mother and sister. She taught the other two girls to get up in the middle of the night and use the bathroom, soon they were train to go up on there own and use the bathroom, Nellie use to change at there diapers including Rodney and Clifton. Now it seem like no one has time for Nellie. The phone rang, it was Bobby, checking to see if she was ok because she was alone, the call snaped Nellie out of her memory of these things but as soon as she got off the phone she went to remembering again she thought about washing so many diapers until she was sick, and there was no pampers, but they was trained to allways be there for each other and to help each other, all they could, the phone again, it was Bobby checking to see if she was ok once more Nellie felt alone, hated, unlove and that her relatives wanted her to get lost. She still had a happyness inside from God Jehovah, she was still studying the bible, and considering getin baptised. After the phone check it was dark, then a real deep feeling of lonlyness came over Nellie so bad until she stared to cry and felt sorry for herself and yell out to Jehovah God I am all by myself in this big world, Oh! father I can't make it like this and when she was about to take a hand fulo of sleeping pills, the phone rang it was one of the lady's Nellie studied the bible with name Bernice Sullervan, she was laughing about something she and her husband James did that day before Nellie realized it she was laughing to they use to talk on the phone a lot but even that has changed, every thing has because when Bernice husband passed away she really took it hard, but she had her children and grand children to help her through this most unbelievable time in there life. Nellie remember all the times when James and Bernice would go on those wonderful cruises, they even sent Nellie acard from the Bohames Island and brough her a tee shirt from one of there trips, Bernice said that they had a ball. All I know is she was so happy and it seem to make me and others happy.

It seem like yesterday because Nellie can not seem to get over her friends lost and her own lost, because she know how they must feel, she have lost so many people that she loved and really need in her life right now. Nellie could take the ones at ease who had something to do with there deaths but God said that vengence is mine and Nellie don't want to do any thing to block her ever lasting life in the kingdom of God. All the lieing on me want do them any good because they can't fool God or put any fear in him like they do us humans, all these peace breakers with friends, and familys break ups. Puting it on someone else, like haveing people you've known for a very long time look at you strange and feel like they have to keep there eyes on you because they have hear lies about how bad you are, the very one putting these lies out may well be the one you should be watching. Sometimes it seem like the pain gets so bad until Nellie can't go on and bear the pain but she believe that God want her to write this book and other teaching work in her Christian organization, and just maybe Nellie can save somebody's life like that sister saved her life, that lonly night, Nellie has faces the hardest times alone, with out her human family companionship she asked herself why? A million dollar word and question, Nellie begain to remember this man that some people thought was a smart man once said to defind the problem is the first step of solveing it. So many people was dieing until Nellie thought that there was a sereal killer walking amoung them watchig, and takeing one at time, stuff like that can make good sane people fearful and not trust others and relatives whom they have knowed all of there life, Nellie wants to run away from this place, but then she thought to herself the only thing that made since was to stay close to God, because she may be falling in there trip, here she is protected by God and people they don't understand, they only know what they have been taught in the world in which they live, meaning that they are copy cats with no feelings, just dead indide but God gives Nellie and others who truly serve him compasstion, for other people feelings and she will go on trying to help any one who will listen to her and believe in God and his power. In 2017, Nellie did get over to her two brothers house it was about two weeks after Christmas, and they set around talking mostly about how each of them were doing and copeing with there illness and takeing care of business, well Nellie was suppose to go over to there house sooner but her pat dog Procious died on the 25th of December, he had been ill for quait some time, she was takeing really good care of him, taking him to the vet, giving him medicine, for about six good years and that seventh year it got really bad he lost his appatite, he would not eat any dog food, the only thing he would eat was chicken quarters, Nellie cooked, which was every day then he lost his appatite for that to, then one day Nellie had gotten some chicken from KFC, and gave the dog Procious some of her KFC chicken and he ate two peices and she started cooking him fried or baked chicken just so he would eat and live a little longer, when she first took him to the vet they said that Procious was the most gentle dog he had ever seen. But nothing could move outside because he was on his job. Nellie can remember how hard it was comeing up and how hard it was geting where she is today, and it still gets hard because the storms come in her life like from every side but she guess you can call her old fashion because she still pray and put her trust in Jehovah and Jesus. She know that a lot of people have forgotten about them and are taught to say there prayers at night or not taught anything at all these day I think that we make to much out of material things and our life is to busy to pray and spend time talking to Jehovah in Jesus name. Nellie had to make a decistion of what was more important to her, God or the things that's possing away, in the world and just by saying that it was God is not all it take to get into his kingdom when it come. It takes really living the life and doing what his word in the bible says, when there's no one around, just you do the right thing, practice what you preach. Sure the 25th of twenty seventeen was sad because of her friend dog Procious passing, she was all ready under a lot of pressure because a couple of months earlyer her husband Bobby had collaped and she had to call 911, and get them to take him to the hospital emengency room and she followed in her car, while they were in his room at the hospital she started to remember when she first started dateing and how hard it was for both of them, Bobby had gotten his devoice and Nellie was in the process of getting a devoice, that was in 1995, when she finally got devoiced and they moved in an appartment together, it was a little rat and roach infected place but they cleaned it. Put rat traps down, sprayed for roaches. At night Nellie would wake up hereing four or five rat traps go off, and in the morning they would clean up.

And the both of them was so happy. Nellie think it was because nobody knew where they stayed. They would have fun watching that little 19 inch color tv, which they got from a rental store, with only regular cable, they watched HBO, staz, cinema and a few other stations, she can remember when she was a child, they only had three stations they didn't have pomputers, cell phones, just there home phones, black and white tvs, radios which Nellie loved cat, they use to play all those reall beautiful records soul music, most of those songs was about how much a man boy, or woman or girl loved there woman or man, or how bad they got hurt then there were songs about getting high, about the injustice of how the whites treated the blacks and other races. She remember one whites band put out a record where the lead singer was singing about sitting getting high with his black cousins, Nellie can not remember the name of this group and if her memory serves her right the ir was other songs maybe not that plain but basically sayin the same thing. People use to call them hippys, this was an errow of change for the whole world especialy the USA, the first change of the style, and everybody wanted to know the truth. Some blacks and whites didn't know the truth until they they saw roots on tv, and some people became angry and hateful, because they could not handle parts of the truth, and some people wanted to make every one esle hate as much as they did. That was back in the 70s the only thing to be said is it was a horrible time for me, but we all know the story that the slaves was suppose to be freed but get this they did not have any education, how could they support themselves? and there familys, so they were freed to modern day salavery because negros had no money or businesses of their own so they had to go back into these white people homes and clean house, cook, wash and raise the kids, some were live in and the others had a house and family to go home to, but they made it through all of this to now.

Negros have colleage degress and good job some have nice houses, and some own their land, and own cars. Afrecan Americans today don't even know how it was for there grand parents and great grand parents back in the 40s, 50s, 60s, even the 70s. Mostly everything blacks was fighting for back then they got. And made it a little better for the younger generation today, so don't waste your time here on earth being angry, just let that go because there's still a long way to go. Remember the Jews were slaves too, Gods people and they are going on, clean up your own neighborhoods because there's should not be any ghettos because we should keep our neighborhoods clean, hold our heads up high, be proud like our grandparent, don't write on the walls, we might be poor but why mess up the little we do have be proud of what's yours and take care of it, a neighborhood is where most people grow and go to the same school and church, played together, where parents know each other, why rob each other, kill and hurt each other? If you are good at motivaing people then charge for it start a little business where people come around you to make them feel better, or if you have a business mine work save your money get a friend that think like you to go into business and open up a store or apartment building, or maybe you arc good at fixing cars, you can do this on your spare time at your own home. Remember just because you are poor don't me an that you have to be sad or nasty, keep your stuff clean as you can, be good to each other and love one another as a people that's going through basisly the same thing work together to have more in life and a better life for yourselves. Nellie looked out of the window she remembered when she and Bobby moved over on Fifth Street, how much Bobby helped his two boys Bobby Jr. and Jerome while they were still in high school, because this meant so much to Bobby to finally be able to do something for his sons whom he loved very much, well that was ok by Nellie cause fathers should take care of the kids like a mother should, and one thing Nellie got to give to Bobby's ex wife Dorlthy, she took care of her kids and she would bring the kids over to see there daddy every week end no matter where he was was staying and visit for a while. But there was other people he knew borrowing money from him and would not pay him back and keep right on doing so, until Nellie asked him who are these floks? They are not relatives, she guess one of them was the woman that left her perfume in his car, Nellie was tied of fighting with him about his lady friends and she was ready for a change, but she did not know how to go about making that change unless she leave him, but she was very ill and had no where to go, now she stay because she have put twenty five good years into this marriage and she has gone through pure pure hell, why lieve now? She still have feelings for him and she thinks that he has feeling for her so they can live the rest of this little time out together and serve God. They can take vacations, and just try to enjoy what's left of this short life in this world, but there have been so many set backs and argarments until it seems like a supernatural thing unclean, but Jesus is still on the throne, the only thing Nellie know how to do is fight the evil power with good and the bible, which is the word of God, but its been so long fighting until she is feeling a little disappointed. Nellie knows that this is a trick of the devil, because she knows that her blessings are near. Then she heard a knot on the door and she said who is it a man voice said Lemont it was Lemont Thomas wanting to get a few dallars that he was short of, she would have not open the door and gave him any thing but Nellie and his mother grew up in the same neighborhood and went to school together so Nellie cracked the door and haded him two dallars he would come every other day so she was use to him asking for a couple of (bones) meaning dollars then he went on his way, Nellie started to remember more about living on Fifth Street, how there were so many things she needed for the house like bath towels, she never seem to get enough, sheets, comforters, curtains, rugs, dish towels and decarations for the house, to make it look and feel homey and cozy. Because Nellie is kind of sickle and stay around the house most of the time. She needed all kinds of personal items but she would still share with others what she could, seem like soneone could help her but maybe she'll get her reward in the kingdom of God, because she sure is trying her best, then a pot boil over she stop thinking and went to see about it she put a little water in the pot and turned the burner down. Then she opened the blinds and started looking out side even the wind now held its breath. A hush of a nticipation swept through the trees, causing the forest creatures to hesitate in their scratchings and birds to faltor in their songs. The woods grew still as everything was pressed under a deep vast silences it came from the east, from wilderness of Pine Bluff, it was like a swelling of the air, a flexing of the ground, as if some enormous power had been hurled in to the earth hundreds of miles away ending tremors through out the land, directly over a country lane, a young squirrel was clamped to the limb of an ancient pecan tree. Tauny hair all over its body now rose and quivered as moss began to prickie under its foot, the deep shuddering stillness flowed through winds. In and amosgst the trees, fur and feather trembled in and out vice grip. The squirrel may have lacked the word for what stored into its mind, but in the same way that it knew of jackal teeth and the lure of high brances, a vague yet frightening awareness was takeing shape. Something many mile distant, something was stirring, changing wakening, then the feeling passed as swiftly as it had arrived and the squirrel let out its breath and looked around. It lifted a paw and examined the mossy bark, sniffed, and turned quick eyes to the ground, to the leaves, to the sky all invain as before, there was no answer to be found. It purged through the air, departing without a trace, but somthing eles now caused little eyes to dart and ears to twitch something quite different. The leaves strewn across the forest lane were begining to quake and shiver. Several pigeons that had been huddling on the ground burst away in all directions with a wild clapping of wings. For the squirrel this was warning enough. It fled accros the branch, disappearing up the peacan tree trunk and into a knot hole as if drawn by a strip. Before it had a chance to push its head out, two jackals was under that tree looking up at him, but that little joker was not momeing down for nothing, Nellie felt a relief, because she wacthed theses little animals mostly every day go through there little rutine of suvival from those really terrofiying larger animals. Then the phone rang it was the school telling Nellie that she had to come pick one of Liz grand kids up because he had got in trouble fighting so Nellie turned the stove off and got into her old car and headed to the school when she got there the teacher had the child siting outside in the cold, Nellie told the teacher that she was wrong for puting him out in the cold no matter what, and where was the boy that he was fighting with? Why only her great nephew had to sit out in the cold? because both of them was fighting, one was no better than the other. One just had more money. This upset Nellie to see so much injustice among the African American race. Then she turned and walked out with out saying another word because she could see that money and friends children got special treatment, if you ask them about this it want do any good, they would only lie and say that's not true, but you can't lie to God. When she got home with the little boy she asked him why was he fighting and he told her that the other kid said something how does it feel to be poor and made fun of him in front of his friends too, and everybody laughed at him the other kid got mad and then pushed him and that was it, because he was raised that talk is cheap, but when someone hit you or push or put there hands on you, protect yourself because you have that right, but first you have to do all you can not to fight. The other kid did not have the friends Lemant had and he said that he could see right through him, the boy was a loner and maybe they did ignore him because he dreeded and talked like a (nored) and did not know how to act and be a friend to them, that he wanted them to look up to him because of his parents money and big find house, and cars, Nellie told Lemant that an it what you got that make you somebody it's your kindness, compastion, and being real to others as well as to yourself and growing into a find human being and it's up to each parent to instill these prioritys in there children. Then the phone rang it was one of Nellie's friends she went to school with they didn't talk long, she just called to tell her that one of there friends from school had passed away, (Oh my God) Nellie could not beleave her ears because so many of her friends and family members had died and she wish that she had spend more time with them, she found some ecuse to get off the phone as soon as possible because she could not let this bad new make her cry. Because her lost of all these people was still fresh at that time. So she told friend her pot was boiling over, and that she would call her back. She set down for a minute and collected her thoughts and began to look out of the window and started to remember when she was out running around like a chicken with its head cut off, back when she was eighteen, nineteen and twenty years old, when she could not stay at home and enjoy the love of her old mother and father, she had to go out everyday to different clubs and juck joints, drinking, smoking dope and danceing all night long until the place would close. She did not feel good about herself, so Mondays she felt so bad throwing up it seem like her guts was going to come up sometime, you would think that this would stop her from drinking and going out so much but as soon she got all that up and out of her, she would bathm, brush her teeth put on sexy cloth and out again doing the same thing. She was not having sex with different men, it was being around party people who look like they were happy and havin fun because she was so sad, depressed and no one understood her or would take the time to listen and get to know her, she lived a fast life, her friends called her Jetfast. She would go around to different clubs and enter there dance contest and win most of them, all she could drink and a pot of money. Every weekend Nellie would go to town and buy herself a sexy outfit to wear to each event, but honey that girl could dance when Elizabeth, Nellie, Margie, Donny, Bonnie, and Peaches walk in a club people would stand up and start clapping, because it was dead with out those pretty girls, they walked like they had been to edited school, people were thrill by there electrified look and personality, look but no touching, proud to be a lady of color. They were respected and loved by the black men, now this was in the seventys, now things have changed because we did not allow them to treat us like fools and call us bithes and hoers, Nellie practiced every day at the club call lous on Six Street not to fore from the loop, in her neck of the wood. Every day she got to see her girl friend Eva whom she called Toostie and Ular may who was the waitress at this club, all the guys and gals she grew up with, just to name a few people like Johnny, her friend Toostie brother, and also Nellie's brother Floyd and his friends Westley, wife (Dale), (Dickey, Candy, Lawranc Mark, Willie C., John Love who was the kindest and thoughful one, Robert, LB, these are the people in the club evday and night also big Mo, and a guy we all call Juke, Buddy and Stamps, let's don't forget Fat Daddy and brother Dume, they all would party, drank and dance every day and this is how Nellie praactice danceing and on the week ends a man name Mr. Dalema Mclemore would drive Liz and

Nellie around all over town to the dance contests. When Nellie was not at the club danceing with her brother Dume, she would be with her two good friends Donny Wilkins and Margie Jones and they would go out to the big nice club in Pine Bluff name PJs and the Elks Club, where school teachers, lawyers, doctors would go to party, people with jobs and money would hang out and get there grove on. There was a not so settle club called the Gala Room, down town on 3rd Street, sometime they had live bands local, and sometime big time stars, people use to come from miles around like Memphis, Little Rock, Mississippi and all those little country towns that surround Pine Bluff, Nellie think they came because of the order and great condition and peace at that particular time in those clubs. Also a club name The Big Place on the west side where Nellie lived and was raised. The proprietor Wiliam and his mother Miss Louceal. Nellie felt a deep pain and sadness because she disappointed her mother, and father, she thought that she had shamed her brother, especially LB, because he paid for her cap and gown for graduation, also he bought her high school ring and she was suppose to go attend Pines Vocational School for nurseing where he and her father Deen set things up. Instead she was running with Margie like crazy, checking out Amand N College which changed to UAPB, today. Nellie had followed hopelessly in love she knew so little about love, until she did not understand that one could fall in love and the other could not be in love with them. On top of all that it was her first love with a young man five years older than she was, she was seventeen when she met this young man with a beautiful smile, and neat Afro, brown skin, act and talked like he was well educated and kind, his name was Otis they would talk for three to four hours on the phone until her daddy or momy tell her to get off and the same with him, but deep down inside Nellie knew that she could never have this boy for her husband, and children's father. Can you imagine a young girl knowing this was forbeted fruit, nothing could ever come of it, that what they had was right then and there, at that time, no one knew what Nellie was thinking or felt, besides the pain, humiliation they were putting her through by pulling the tricks of time, but God will be the judge and they have to stand before God the same as Nellie, but even this is not going to beat her out of the oppertunity for the kingdom of God, because Nellie has put everything, her whole life in God's hands, she can't go back, so she has to go on as long as God let her, you see it don't take much to please Nellie, the joys that are free in life most of the time, but we all know that we need money to live in weaked system of things, to pay our bills to put food on the table and to take care of your family's needs and wants. There was a clap of thuder in the sky, Nellie came out of the day dream, then went to take care of her pats, to feed and bath them. After that she thought about all of the suffering and horrible things she went though, how she would never wish these things on the one that cause most of this upon her, even her worse enemy, and she could never treat them as bad as they treated her. But what's so bad about it all? She belive that the few that's left alive is still trying to hinder and hurt her, all of this could have destroyed Nellie and it allmost did, if she didn't remember that her decistions are the cause for her own condition in life. She had to start changing her own life with the help of the good Lord, she has a style of her own by not leting some people in her house or out side her house control her thinking or how she feels. Nellie knew that what you respect? You will attract respect and healing. You can feel confustion, sickness, or no respect and abuse, whatever is missing in your life, something that you valued, and what you don't have in intellegents you can make up with your respect and attitude, you can only learn best from someone you admire. What you make happen for others God will make happen for you. Do unto others as they should do unto you, the secret of your future is hidden in your daily routine. Something you are doin daily is affecthing your future, if you succeed it will be because of a daily habbit or routine, money is somctime a reward for solveing problems, your rewards in life are decided by the kinds of deeds you sow. If you insist on takeing something God did not give you, he will take back something that he gave you. An uncommon deed will allways create a uncommon harvest, out of a bad time in your life, what you sow to God is magnified back, it can be a seed of minding God because he spoke it in the bible, you see routine and studying the bible for yourself and applying these things he told you to do in your life is very important. Seek first the kingdom of God and all these other things will be added to your life because every thing you need to have success is within you. And when you get blessings from God, remember to be humble, kind, respectful to other people, who do not have as much as you, because money does not make you better or above people, or the ones who are still trying to find theres. Nellie had to wash, sweep, make breakfast, wash dishes, and mop kitchen floor. She was very tied so she took nape, after she woke up it was just enough time to have a bite to eat with Bobby before he went to work, after he left she begain to think about when she came back to Pine Bluff one time after being away for ten years. She had driven straight through with her best friend Carl from Washington DC, with his son David, now they were back in Pine Bluff, David was no longer fidgeting. He was no longer peering impatiently out the window. He was slumped in the passenger seat, his eyes in a level with the bottom edge of the rolled up window. Nellie was thinking how out of place she felt comeing back into the place she was raised and grew up in. How sometime you have to be an outcast with people in order to be a incast with God, you have to decide do I please the God who gave me life? or do I please the God who really love me? or should I please people who should be trying to please God the same as me. your appreciation should not be to a man of God but to God himself. Nellie asked David what's wrong? Daved adjust cap. He always wore the bill in back, the popular look in DC. Now he reversed it, slipping the bill lower over his face. David? not in okay? Nellie beleived she hadn't adopted that impatient tone with her mother until she'd been at least thiteen kids grew up faster today. David had mastered the arrogant inflections of adolescence within two weeks of moving in with Carl after his mother died. Nothing had changed, not bribery, not spoiling him and not getting tough with him, which had come hard with a grieving boy, you don't look very happy to be here after being so all fired eager to come back, Carl said. David ignored them. The silent treatment was David's favorite methed of dealing with his god mother, Nellie smothered a sigh and kept driving. Nellie's first impression of her home town hypnotized her. An American flag still flutted in front of the library, as it had e very clear day durning her childhood. The book store, the candy store, the old hardware store all looked the same. In fact, the brick buildings had changed little since they were constructed along Ridge Lane in the nineteen twentys. The main treet of town curved and rolled, gently following the terra in, hugging the side of the wooded hill that rose toward the main land mark, heritage manor. The town had grown up more than a century earlier around the gracious old resort and spa, its progress ebbing and flowing with changes in society and the economy buildings harking back to the previous century were still scattered among the other businesses. The Victorian house next to the library had been spruced up, though three cradles sat in a row on the broad porch, with an enormous Siamese cat serving as sentry, triplets in Pine Bluff? Nellie wondered if the mother was someone she knew. Some woman she'd been to high school with, maybe getting nervous as the biological clock ticked, trying fertility drugs and ending up hitting a grand slam. Nellie turned her imagination off it was an old habit of hers, the way she intertained herself, she invented lives for the people she saw and then didn't feel quite as lonely. And it was better safer than getting close to real people, findin out who they really were, what their real stories were. Because eventually real people also wanted to know her real story, and that was always when the friendships cooled, people asking questions over a beer after work. Where was she from? How had she made it to Washington, DC? Husband? Kids? Family? And Sabashiean: always backed off, shut them out, refused to get close. Weaving tales about strangers was easier than negotiating the land mines in her own past. Carl was driveing, he turned off university on to Pullen Street, made the second left between the high school and a daycare center. He held his breath. The cries and gigles of the children from the daycare grew more distant. Then an old house set back from the street came into view. It looked shabbier and smaller than he remembered. The white clap board was dingy, in need of painting. The door of the screened porch hung slightly, shrubs grew up over the windows. Where the hell was Herbert? Carl said and she and Carl wondered. Carl hoped his younger brother hadn't let the place fall into this kind of disrepair before their mother died. Why are we here? David sat up in his seat, suddenly interested as his father Carl pulled the pickup into the rutted gravel drive. This isn't a Unt Thelmas we're not going to Thelmas. Carl killed the engine and gave the hand brake a yank. Nellie guessed from Carl mothers letters that she barely knew her grand son. But it galled Carl to realize David didn't even know where she'd lived. This was grandma Marian's place. David kicked the dash with the expensive sneakers that represented one of Carl's attempts at bribery, I am not gonna live here. This isn't home. I wanna go home Nellie felt her temper rising on a wave of wounded feelings, but she shoved it down and out of the way. Anger wasn't the answer. It wasn't David's fault that Carl's ex wife Karlar and no doubt her sister had raised him to think of the father and god mother Nellie as some kind of low life. It wasn't David's fault, he hated Nellie and father. That didn't make it hurt any less. That hadn't made it any easier to live with the boys sullenness these past nine months. Nellie opened the truck door and got out. This home. You got your way and we're back in Pine Bluff, and that's as close as it's going to get to the way things used to be. She saw the boy slower lip start to tremble and ached to take him into her arms and comfort him. But she wasn't up for the rejection she knew would follow???

Come on, son, Carl said let's unload. For once at least David didn't tell him not to call him son. Unloading the back of the truck didn't take long even with a foot dragging eight year old as helper. None of the furniture in there DC. Apartment had been worth hanging on to, so they'd loaded up cloths and little else. Nellie had hoped the house where David's father grew up might still be full of David's grandmothers furniture, her dishes, her pots and pans. She wasn't disappointed about that. What she had't expected, however, was that the house would also be full of dust and cobwebs and signs the squirrels had made themselves at home. There was no sign that David's Uncle Herbert had even been in the house since their mother died years earlier Carl ground his teeth together to keep from swearing. Mr. Butler, the old attorney who had contacted Nellie two years ago about the inheritance which had consisted of the old house, back taxes and little else had assured Carl and Nellie that Herbert still lived in Pine Bluff. Nellie had assumed David's fathers brother

Herbert would look after things. She'd abviously been wrong. It's all dirty, David said petulantly. We can't live here. Carl stuck his head in the kitchen pantry. Brooms, mops, cleanser. Carl I think we can manage. I wanna go to my Aunt Thel

Ma's, Carl ignored his son's whine. David looked in the refrigerator. No food. Carl handed him a spray bottle and the bucket of rags and sponges that were right where Marian had always kept them, in the back of the pantry. Start on the refrigerator, then. "Me? You." While David grumbled and ran water into the bucket, Nellie roamed the house. The old fashioned fleur wall paper in the living room was the same as were the television and the old upright pinano Marian had played again after her mother Mrs. Vera Brooks passed away. The furniture was covered by dingy sheets, the outlines looked familiar the old comeback sofa, a recliner, the big swivel rocker where his mother seldom sat for more than ten minutes without thinking of one more chore that needed tending. Carl shook off the nostalgia. He'd leave the sheets in place until the worst of the dust was gone. He continued to the bedroom. His mother's clothes still hung in her closet. They were dreary, gray, with dust, reminding him of the way Marian face had also gone gray after Clarl's problems worse, even then after Carl father had died. The weight of her grief had seemed to collect on her face, dragging down the flesh and leeching it of color and life. Fifty seven, that was how old she'd been when she died. Too young to be old and broken from so much misery. "Damn! Carl shoved the closet shut and went on to the next room. In the room he had shared with his brother, all signs of his existence had been obliterated. He moved past it quickly. In the cramped bathroom, with its old claw footed tub, he caught a glimpse of pink crocheted covers fitted over the box of tissues and the extra roll of toilet paper. Water dripped into the tub from the leaky faucet, wearing away the porcelain and leaving a rusty spot beside the drain. Carl wished he could think of someone to ask for reassurance (so did Nellie) that they have done the right thing, by bringing his son back here. He needed some body to tell him everything would work out all right. But there was nobody. There had been nobody for too long, he should be used to it by now. By bedtime, the two of them had lifted the worst of grime in the two bedrooms and the kitchen. They went for take out at a place called the tex a tavern. Carl hoped no one would notice or remember him. The clientele in the dimly lit restaurant had the look of tourists khakis and low polp shirts, walkin shoes and visors. He escaped unrecognized with their tacos and soft drinks. They ate in silence, went to bed in silence and had breakfast in silence the next morning the silence ended only when Carl explained to David that he would be in rolling in school that morning. Nellie had gone over to her mother's house to stay because she only got a ride back home with them. David asked why? because you're eight years old, eight year olds go to school. I got just here. I should have a week off. Or two. When David had arrived in Washington, DC. Still raw from his mother's Death, Carl had kept his son home for a week before inrolling him in school. His plan had been to comfort his son, to give him time to get accustomed to his new surroundings. He'd also hoped to get to know the boy's whose mother had taken him away when he was seventeen months old. He had'nd seen David since, because Janet had refused to let him visit on Carl's tuf, she'd also done the one thing quaranteed to keep Carl at a distance she had returned to Pine Bluff. The first week of his reunion with Carl hadn'd panned out. David would accept no comfort, remained wary, rejected his fathers attempts to get to know him, Carl had assumed all of that would change with time, but he'd been wrong. David was stubborn and unbending. At least in the months they'd been together, David had learned that arguing with his father was pointless. When it became clear the first morning in Pine Bluff that enrolling in school was not up for debate, he trudged along behide his father, the silence between them restored. Carl didn't like the startled looks from the women behind the desk in the office at the elementary school. He didn't like the nudge one of them gave the other as she pointed out his name on the paper work he'd filled out for David. He didn't like the way they pursed their lips and avoided his eyes. Yep, nothing had changed in Pine Bluff Arkansas. When the proccess was finished and David was sittin in a roomful of third greaders Carl walked out the front door. The ancient Oak Street. What few cars came through the intersection of old Oak Street. Circled it carefully, bumping over the roots that buckled the pavement. The tree had been there longer than the brick school or the stone church or the municipal parking lot on the corners. It had been there longer than anyone still alive in Pine Bluff, and the town had long since decided it was wrong to do anything but work around something that enduring. Carl had always thought that was a virtue, until he realized that other attuides in the small town could be just as enduring. He knew what he had to do. He knew what he'd come back to do. Just as Nellie knew what she come back to do and what she had to do. There was no other way to bring up Carl son here. No other way to make peace with their past. They had to prove all wrong. The real estate office was different and the old diner had changed hands, it appeared. Things looked somewhat more somewhat more prosperous, but it was only here the people who looked substantially different. He didn't recognize a single soul, which he supposed was no surprise. Twenty years change people much more than it change buildings and landscopes. That didn't stop Nellie or Carl from feeling certain that everyone passed recognize them. Though

Carl imagined distrust and suspicion in the eyes of everyone be saw. Did they remember the trial that ruine his life? If they don't now, they will soon enough. The phone rang broke Nellie out of her day dream of twenty years ago. It was Bobby checking in with her before he would get off o work, Bobby told Nellie that he found a wallet with two hundred dollars inside, and he had taken the wallet to the lost and found and checked back on it afew minutes ago and someone had claimed it and the lady that helped find the owner told Bobby that it looked like they really needed that money too, but Bobby had done the right Christian thing, it made her proud of him because she would have done the same, but not all way Nellie can remember when she and Bobby would have put that money in their pockets and maybe felt a little guilty, but soon that would have disappeared. Just like most sinful things we do. Then soon if you are not careful you will be doing more and more of sin, it can turn into steeling biger things, even robbery, get caught and sent to jail. Maybe even lieving a family behind suffering, awoman need of a husband and children in need of a father, can make a good women go out doing things unlady like. Things like saleing her precious body and even murder only to put food on the table to feed her and children, to put a roof over there heads, all this because of one sin lending to others and destroing a whole family of good people, how awful this sounds even thinking about it, but this could happen, even when a man or woman have sex with someone besides their husband or wife, they could come down with some kind of desease, life takeing or cureable how will they explain to their spouse. How it happened? Maybe there partner won't ever trust them again and they are to hurt and want out of the marriage, when all of this could have been avoided by not doing the crime at all, Bobby said hello Nellie are you there? Broke her thinking, yes she said I am real proud of you. Those people are so blessed to have a superviser like you one who can set a really good example for them. Bobby said well it wasn't hard to do, I'll call you before I leive for home, ok I'll see you then and hung up the phone and ran him a bubble bath then she set the table with home made chicken wings soup with corn bread and strawberry cake. When Bobby came in the house five days a week, he would go to the bath room take a bath, put on clean pjs and come out to eat his dinner because every night for eight years he knew that it would be there just like that because his wife Nellie was going to see to it being like that for him because she knew that he was very tied and hungry and needed to be pampered after work. But still there was to much argueing between them, just irritated with each other. Money was't right, in need of so many, had to help family members and staying broke, they took up lots of stuff on their credit cards and was in debt, so yea hurtful things were said by both of them. But they didn't physically hurt each other. Which is good because you here about couples shooting or cuting each other to death. It's so sad when you here it on the news or read in the new paper. Bobby told Nellie that he was going to see if he could take two weeks off for vacation because he was having a hard time greving when his Uncle Earnest died, reminded Nellie of a two week stay in this place that was supposed to heal the gaping hole in her heart and save her career? Sure. If she was lucky, maybe she'd get a band aid out of the deal. Gravel crunched and popped beneath the tires a Nellie eased the convertible to a stop. Just ahead, bright, multi colored sign arced over the dirt road. Campfire fly wishes. A place full of miracles, she'd been told. She could certainly use one of those. But she wouldn't hold her breath, her hands trembled, and Nellie gripped the steering wheel harder, turning her knuckles white. If her boss in cahoots with her father hadn't insisted, she wouldn't be here, facing something she wasn't certain she'd ever be ready to face. The hot, mid July sun made her glad she'd put the top down, the humid air carried the soundeds of chirping birds and rustling leaves. She closed her eyes and inhaled deeply, catching the scent of freshly mowed grass. The smells and sounds of summer vacation. If she tried hard enough, she could make believe that this summer vacation would be the way it always had been a time of joy and peace, of fireflies, bare feet and children laughter, of no lesson plans, and time with her family, with her son. But summer would never be like that again. A blaring horn jolted her from her reverie. Nellie glanced in the rearview mirror to see a silver SUV practically on her bumper. The driver offered her a friendly wave, then leaned out his window. "Is anything wrong? more like everything. But somehow she'd got through this. She eased the convertable into gear and slowly traveled the dirt lane steering carefully around the potholes still filled with rain water. On her left, she saw the stables. Several chestnut horses stamped their hoove and nickered as she passed. A large field the source of the grassy smell appeared next. It had the markings of a baseball diamond and a soccer field. All in all, the place looked remarkably like the brochure her principal had forced on her, remarkably like any other summer camp she'd ever attended or seen pictures of except for the helipad at the far end of the field. That one detail reminded her this was unlike those other camps. This one catered to kids who'd had organ transplants and their families. Since the camp was more than an hours drive north of Pittsburgh, Pennsylvania, the helipad probably reassured parents that competent medical help was only a short flight away just in case. Nellie's throat tightened and she blinked a few times. A fleeting glance in the mirror showed the SUV still following closely. Which meant a U turn and quick getaway were out of the question. But escaping wasn't an option, anyway Nellie had to consider her career. It was all she had left. The camps main building a large, rambling, wood sided structure came into view. She chose a parking space near the front doors. The SUV slipped into the slot beside her. Childish laughter of her summer fantasy components floated to her ears as a family exited the building, she thought the families weren't cam arriving until tomorrow? Maybe they wern't campers. Both children appeared robust and energetic as they avorted along the side walk, not what she imagined a transplant child would look like. Nellie grabbed the leather satchel from the passenger seat and rummaged through its contents. Yanking out the appropriate file, she searched for the letter of confirmation from the camps owners. The wind swirled down and lifted the papers into the air. "Sugar cookies!" She launched herself across the seat after them, managing to land on all but one before they flew away. A throatt, masculine chuckle made her glance up. Such language, the SUV driver gently chiled, yet tempered with grace. I'd give that dive a nine. He offered her the errant sheet of paper. Here's the one you missed. Nellie's cheeks warmed, and she straightened up, then ran a hand over her hair as she studied him. A dimple cleaned his angular chin. Short brown hair, the color of rich coffee. Eyes the color of melted caramel. Broad shoulders that tapered down to a narrow waist. He shook the page. Do you want this back, or should I let the breeze have it, after all? Her cheeks flamed hotter as she accepted the paper.

Thanks." She scanned the sheet. Oh, no. She glanced back at the man who was caressing the top of her passenger door. What's today? Sunday. He looked down at her. Nice car. Oh no, sun day? Are you sure? Yes I'm sure. He extended his hand to her. I'm Carlos. And I'm late! Nellie stuffed the papers back into the folder. This isn't happening. How could she have messed up so badly? Granted, once school let out for the year, one day seemed the same as the next. But to actually show up on the wrong day? She really didn't want to be here. Maybe this was her subconscious way of avoiding it, if your subconscious gets you fired, what then? Panic tightened her throat. She shifted across the seat and jumped from the car, nice to meet you." Carlos McClain found himself staring as the woman dashed up the side walk. She was thin almost to thin but that didn't.

She was thin almost to thin but that didn't negate a gently curved and perfectly proportioned rear. Her determined march displayed purpose and a little bit of panic, there was no seductive sashaying, or slinking, and yet he couldn't pull his attention from the seat of her well fitting white shorts. Daddy? "If ever there was a word was a word designed to burst the bubble of erotic visions, that was it. But then, his girl was worth the sacrifices he made, a normal love life being one of them. Fantasy was about all he could manage. Caring for her and running his psychology practice took all his time. Carlos turned to face the open window of the SUV and his daughter. Yeah, tiger? Who was that lady? Rose awake from her short nap, leaned out, craning her neck to look around him. He glanced over his shoulder for a final peek as the front door swung shut behind the delightful rear. I don't know." She has pretty hair. Carlos stiffed a chuckle. There in lay the diffence between a thirty seven year old male and an eight year old little girl. Although sometimes his daughter seemed far older than he was. Yes she does, sweetie. Now, are you ready to camp? Iwa's born ready. "What ever you say, Unsinkable." Da_a_ad." Rose eyes narrowed. You promised not to call me that while we were here. I'm not a baby anymore. He stopped himself from telling her she'd always be his baby. Running a fingertip across her cheek. He marveled at the healthy pink flush in her skin. No, you're not. He pressed gently on her freckle covered nose. But you'll always be the unsinkable Rose McClain. If I'm so unsinkable, then why don't you let me do all the things I want to? Like go to camp by myself? Like a normal kid. Carlos heard the qualifier his daughter lift unvoiced. Rose you the reason." They do have camps that will take a transplant kid by themselves, you know. Not like this one, where the family comes along. Camps that aren't just about in our own backyard, too." A thirty-five minute ride from home wasn't enough to provide the adventure she craved, I know. But you're not old enough. Maybe next year. He ignored the prickling sensation at the back of his neck. Planning for next summer seemed incredible, a far cry from last summer most of which he and Rose had spent at childrens hospital. With good luck and good management, she'd have a next year. He'd spent a lot of her life praying. And he'd damn near lost her. Her new heart had come just in time. That had been last September almost a year ago. His surgeon had worried that she wasn't going to be strong enough to survive the transplant. Now, if he could just keep her new heart healthy. A dazzling smile brightened Rose's face, but a tiny trace of skepticism showed in her hazel eyes. Really, Dad? Next year I can camp by myself? Maybe. I'll think about it. Let's see how this year goes first, huh? She leaned farther out and wrapped her arms around his neck. I love you!" Carlos pulled her the rest of the way out of window. I love you, too. After a quick hug, he set her on her feet and took her by the hand now, let's go see about our cabin. Nellie went to see her cabin also I'm afraid I assigned your cabin to someone else, dear. Had to separate a pair of volunteer women who don't seem to get along. Trudy brown, the camp director, rose from her wooden swivel chair and perched on the front edge of the desk. A rotating fan hummed on the top of an oak filing cabinet, providing some relief from the summer heat. Don and I figured you'd changed your mind. We both know Jerry pretty much forced you to come. Nellie toyed with the handle of her bag. Well if you've been friends with Jerry for as many years as he says, then you know once he makes up his mind, there's no changing it. Her principals had taken extensive lessons from her father. And when the two men best friends ever since her father had saved Jerry's life by carrying him on broken ankles crashed banded together, people found themselves doing things they really didn't want to. Like getting married or coming here. Trudy shook her head and made a sympathetic tsking noise. She had a warm but weather red face and a short, barrel shaped body. But her orange hair and loudd tie dyed shirt, paired with faded bell bottom jeans made the woman resemble aunt bee from the old television show, warped through wood stock. Jerry says you're a wonderful teacher, and he's very worried about you. Uh huh. "Are you sure you want to be here?" Something in the way she asked made Nellie wonder if the camp director was the one having second thoughts. And frankly, Nellie didn't blame her. Who knew what Jerry had told her? Did he mention the confusion? We'll, after showing up on the wrong day, that one ought to be clear. The misplaced plan books? The report cards not finished on time? The thousand little details that slipped her mind of late? She signed. I don't have a choice, Mrs. Brown." Trudy, the woman admonished. Trudy. Yes right. Nellie shifted in the chair, the bare skin of her thighs unsticking from the wooden surface with an embarrassing sucking noise. I've been a teacher for ten years, and loved every minute of it.

Without my career to keep me occupied this past year, I'm sure I'd have been admitted to the funny farm by now. She dropped her voice to a whispera and looked down at the faded tile floor. Since I lost Daniel, it's been my only reason to get out of bed each morning. "But it's hard to be an effective teacher, dear, if you don't like being around children anymore." Nellie whipped her head up and met Trudy's frank gaze. Is that what Jerry said? That's not it at all. I love kids. It's just" It's just what? It's just hard, that's all Nellie rose from the chair to wander across the office. Sheets of paper with various schedules cluttered a bulletin board. Around the edges, photos of smiling children advertised the joys of summer camp. A little boys with sun streaked brown hair and sparkling blue eyes caught her attention. How Daniel would have loved camp, the horses and the swimming, the boating. A heaviness invaded her chest icy fingers squeezed her heart like the play doh Daniel had loved. Nellie closed her eyes and swallowed hard. It's okay to miss him." Trudy said softly from near her shoulder. Eyes flashing open, Nellie stepped to the side. And leaned against the windowsill. She didn't want to discuss it with a strange woman, a woman whose report to Jerry at the end of the session would determine whether Nellie had a career or not. He'll, she didn't want to talkabout it with anyone. But she was going to have to play the game if she wanted to keep teaching second graders. If the administration, particularly Jerry's boss, the superintendent, didn't think she could handle her job and her grief over losing Daniel, they'd insist she take a medical leave of absence. Which would leave her with nothing to distract her from the pain. Somehow, Nellie had to convince this woman that she could get close to kids, that she was still a good teacher. Trudy, is there some place else I could bunk, since you've reassigned my cabin? You're sure you want to stay? The woman's green eyes expressed her reservation.

Yes. I want to stay. Good, I'm so glad! There was genvine warmth in Trudy's voice. I've got an empty cabin over in the family loop. The parents here will treat you as a sort of hero you're not going to tell them? Trudy studied her intently for a moment, then shoot her head. I hoped you would. Nellie tried not to let her dismay show. The other woman continued, you're not just here to help us with the kids. You're here because Jerry thinks and Don and I agree that seeing the kind of miracles that can come from tragedy will help you. Don't got a PhD. In counseling, and he runs support groups for the parents, and we'd love for you to sit in on some of them. "I...I don't know if I can. I don't think I want people to know." Well, in your own time. Come on, I'll show you where your cabin is." Nellie let the camp director lead her from the office. She left numb as she methodically placed one foot in front of the other. The funny smoke from Trudy's hippie past had apparently added a few too many of the womans brain cells. What else would explain the fact that she expected Nellie to tell the parents of transplant children that Daniel, her sweet four and a half year old son, her only child, had been an organ donor? Oh, Dad, isn't it great? Rose skipped up the steps to the bright blue cabin, the second to last one in the row. A nearly identical structure this one painted a shade of yellow that reminded Carlos of corn on the cob and melted butter sat to his right. The dirt road dead ended in front of it. He dragged the suitcases from the back of the SUV and followed his daughter. It's very nice. Wait for me." He gritted his teeth at the twinge in his right shoulder, compliments of Rose bag. How many clothes did an eight year old need for camp? What else did she have stashed in the case.? Books more than likely. Rose was a avid reader. She certainly had plenty of time in her short life to cultivate the hobby. But how many books did it take to make a suitcase over the weight limit for some small bridges? He looked around. Tall trees some pine, most hardwood filled the area across from the cabin. Rose ran her hand across a set of purple metal wind chimes near the front door, setting off a series of melodic tinkling sounds. Several hundred feet behind the cozy wooden structure, wooden structure a lake beckoned, small ripples slapping gently against the shore. The peacefulness of the place invited serious relaxation. If he was lucky, maybe there was a hammock near by. He had't had areal vacation since before Rose was born. Dad!

Come on, hurry up!." I'm coming he muttered, following his daughter up the steps. The small screened porch contained two folding lawn chairs and a wooden coat tree. Carlos dropped the luggage and searched his pocket for a key. Rose plastered her nose against the window. I can't open it with you in the way, Sweetheart. She stepped aside to let him unlock the door, then rushed in ahead of him dodging the table and four chairs near the front windows. Carlos walked past the efficiency kitchen and tossed his carry on on the blue couch in front of the fire place. Rose popped out of a door on the far end of the living room. I want this bedroom, Dad. I can see the lake from the window! Carlos fished a can of disinfectant spray from his bag, returned to the porch to pick up Rose's suit case and headed into the room she had chosen. After depositiong the hernia maker on a luggage stand, he began to spray the White wicker furniture. Rose turned at hiss of the can. Dad! Can't you give it a break? Jeez. She threw open the window. That stuff reeks. The second window in the room resisted, but with a grunt, she shoved it halfway up. Germs are the enemy, yeah, I know. Carlos nodded. With an immune suppressed child, he couldn't take germs lightly. The medication that prevented Rose's immune system from attacking her new heart also left her susceptible to sicknesses other kids could brush right off. A summer cold or a virus could turn into something serious, even life threatening, for Rose. Pins and needles jabbed at the back of his neck, and his shoulder muscles tightened at the thought. Stop complaining. Unpack your cloths, then I wanted you to lied own for a little while. He held up his hand to forestall the whine he saw coming. Tonight after dinner there's a bonfire to welcome everyone, and you'll probably be up late. So, take your pick. Lie down now for a while, or leave the party early. She rolled her eyes at him. Okay, you win. That's my girl. I'm going to get the rest of the stubb out of the car. Rose began unpacking as he headed out. Several large hard cover books appeared from the depths of her bag and Carlos groaned. Next time do you old dad a favor and bring paperbacks, would you, Tiger? She grinned at him, eyes shining. You're not old, dad. You're just slightly used." Oh, thanks a lot. Was that supposed to be a compliment? If so, you need to work on it a little more. Slightly used. Oh, thanks a lot. Was that supposed to be a compliment? If so, you need to work on it, slightly used? He pondered the words as he thudded down the cottage steps. Sometimes badly used felt more like it. His exwife, Tiffany, who rarely contacted their daughter, was responsible for most of that. And Rose's medical condition had also contributed to the battering he'd taken. All the surgeries she'd needed as the doctors tried to correct her birth defect. All the unknowns. Finally having to put her on the transplant list. And then, the waiting. It was so hard to live your life not knowing if this day would be your childs last. Tiffany hadn'd even tried. She'd bolted by the time Rose was five months old and fled to the west coast. Sunlight glinted off the polished black surface of a car at the yellow cottage. Carlos blinked, then raised his hand to shield his eyes. It was the GTO convertible belonging to the flustered black hair woman. A woman shouldn't be driving it a classic muscle car no matter how good she looked in a pair of tight shorts. It was a man's car. Testosterone and leaded fuel. If the P.C. police knew his thoughts, he'd lose his psychologist license for sure. But he had to get a closer look at it again. Beting back a grin and the urage to grunt like Tim Allen, he strolled down the dirt lane, one eye on the car, the other on the cabin. When the owner didn't appear, he lost himself in admiration of the machine of his dreams, inspecting it closely from one end to the other. Bent over the engine some time later, he became aware of the faint scent of lemon and the distinct feeling of warmth behind him. A quick glance over his shoulder confirmed his suspicion. Busted. Don't you know it's rude to get under somones hood without permission? Carlos straightened, then turned, finding himself close enough to touch the nameless woman. We'll." She propped her fists on her hips and eyed him the same way he did Rose when he caught her up to no good. He forced a casual grain and stole a few seconds of observation time. Her shoulder length corn silk hair had been pulled back into a ponytail, and in the bright sunlight, he notice small lines around her eyes and mouth, smile lines. Obviously this was a woman with with a sense of humor. Only she wasn't smileing now. Some time it's easier to ask forgiveness than it is permisstion he said. One corner of her mouth twited, then she shook her head. So you're sorry you're under my hood? Could he cox that ting twitch into a full blown grin? I'm sotry if I made you mad. But I'm not sorry I'm under your hood. Her eyes widened, and she drew a sharp breath. With another shake of her head, she stepped back, clearly delineating the line he'd inadvertenly crossed when he turned to face her. Men. You're all the same aah, so you're barroring some hostilityt toward my entire gender. As a psychologist who counseled many couples and familys, he should know. He often had a ring side seat for the battle between the sexes. He stole a quick look at her left-hand. No wedding ring, but that didn't nesessarily mean any thing. This is a great car, and I couldn't resist checking it out. He gestured (to ward) the engine. Is that a four hundred turbo trannie? She shrugged. I don't know, you don't know? You own this terrific car, and you don't know? What's under her hood? No I don't really care. Either. It get me where I want to go, and that's all that matters. Carlos closed his mouth to stop it from gaging. After several seconds, he found his voice again. You want to sell it? Her eyes narrowed. She freed the prop stick and slammed the hood, forcing him backward. It's not for sale. Trust me, you don't have enough money to buy it. Try me.

No. There are some things money can't buy, and this car is one of them. A gift from a man friend? He asked. Though how any man would part with a car like this was beyond him. He hollow chuckle lacked humor. In a manner of speaking. This car belonged to my ex husband. Now it belong to me. She ran a palm over the hood, then slapped it soundly. Carlos winced classic displaced aggression. Not too fond of him, then, are you? She looked back up at him. You know the nick name for this car. Carlos? He nodded. Goat. Right. Let's just say I got Romans goat in the divorce settlement. She folled her arms across her chest, as though daring him to make something of it. What a tough cookie. Wonder what else she took the poor sucker for? He glanced at the GTO again. There's no way I'd have let my ex wife end up with a car like this. No way in hell. She'd gotten enough of his money, but a car like this he'd have fought for. Just like he would have fought for Rose if he'd had to. But then, Tiffany hadn't wanted Rose, couldn't deal with Rose's condition, with the ever present risk of losing her, with the hospital and doctors. The woman's ghost of a smile disappeared, and she lowered her hands to her sides. I didn't think I'd get it, either. But when a man wants his freedom badly enough, he'll give up just about anything. Including his most prized possession. She kicked the tire. I didn't aske for anything else. Not alimony, nothing. Just this stupid car. She brushed her sneaker in the loose dirt around the wheel. A small way to make him pay. The tough cookie had been replaced by a woman with obvious wounds. Experience told him there was a lot more to the story than the exchange of a car for freedom. Ouch. I'm sorry. Nellie glanced up from the gravel she'd been scuffing with her toe. Don't be so hard on yourself, I'm not. He played, and he paid. Although, there had been a far greater cost to his playin a cost he'd never be able to compensate for. If he hadn't been so distracted by his new squeese, maybe Daniel would still be alive. So you got his goat, but didn't take him for a ride? Nope just wanted his car. You know, hit him where it hurts? Remind me not to mess with you. He smiled broadly at her, showing a solitary dimple deep in his right cheek paired with the cleft in his chin, it made him even more attractive. We never did finish our introductions. He held out his hand. Since we're going to be neighbors for the next two weeks, maybe we should try again. I'm Carlos McClain. Nellie. Nellie Bush. A pleasure to meet you. Nellie. He gave her fingers a light squeeze, then let go. My daughter, Rose, had a heart transplant a year ago in September. How about you? Daughter? Heart transplant? She hadn't seen a child in the back of his car but then the windows were tinted. She'd gotten the impression he was a single guy without a family, another employee stuck at the far reaches of the family cabin loop due to one of Trudy's assignment mix ups. But that wasn't the case. This man had one of those walking miracles she'd been sent here to see. A miracle born of a tragedy like hers. Nellie? She looked back up into those soft brown eyes, which now shone with concern. Uh, I I'm here no kids? Damn. Now he'd really done it. Her nose tingled as though someone had poured soda into it, her eyes misted over, she pinched the bridge of her nose hard and struggled for composure. I have to go. I have lesson plans to write up. She turned on her heel and headed for her cabin. In her mind she could hear her fathers clipped voice barking the phrase he'd used so often durning her childhood. Good little soldiers don't cry. Chin left and good looks be damned, Carlos McClain was nothing but trouble with his miracle child and probing questions. She'd survived a heart defect and a transplant, but figured she'd eventually die of embarrassment. Caused by her father. He could be such a dork. Rose crossed her eyes and stuck out her tongue at his back as he carried their dinner trays to the garbage cans on the far side of the dining hall. I saw that, a soft voice with a faint southrn accent drawled. What's he done now? Rose spun on the bench, then jumped to her feet, aah! Cherry! She flug her arms around her friend and squeezed her tight. You made it! I told you I was coming. Cherry wiggled from the embrace then plopped down at the table. Yeah, but your biopsy was last week. You were supposed to call me. Rose frowned at the other girl. Rejection rights after her transplant a year ago had almost killed Cherry. How was it? I'm here aren't I? Relief washed through her. No rejects? Clean as baby's butt. Cherry grinned and grabbed Rose's hand. During a bath, that is. The two girls giggled. You should know Rose said. What's it like having a new baby around? Cherry wrinkled her nose. Noisy, stinky and usually wet at both ends. She tugged rose down onto the seat next to her and whispered in her ear, but I'll tell you one thing. It sure gives my mom something better to do than fuss over me all the time. Jeez, I wish dad had something better to do. You still didn't tell me what he did this time. Rose swiveled her to check on her father's return. He was still on the far side of the room, talking to a short lady with orange hair, orange? That was even worse than her own red mop. Rose turned back to her friends. The usual. Eat this healthy food. Take a nape. Don't over do it. Wash those hands. Oh, and my very favorite, the disinfectant spray you know, I could clobber the people who invented disinfectant wipes. Dad wiped down the table and bench when we got here. O mi God. How embarrassing. Even my mom's not that bad. Tell me about it. Rose searched the dining hall. Where is your mom? I want to see the baby. She's at our cabin, feeding him. You come by yourself? Yeah, so? I'm ten I can come to the dining hall without getting lost. Must be nice, Rose muttered. Look, your dad will back off a little when you're older. Sure. Maybe when I go to high school. Guilt pocked at her. Her dad loved her and was only trying to protect and take care of her. He was always there when she needed him. He just hadn't learned to let go when she didn't. If he had his way, she'd still have training wheels on her bike. Let me ask him if we can go to your cabin. Rose jumped up, slamming into someone. Oh, no! watch out. The woman's dinner tray hovered just over Rose's head and she fumbled with it, just barely saving it from crashing to the floor. The contents of a tall plastic glass sloshed over the top and spattered the tray, the woman's meal and her pretty pink shirt. I'm sorry! Rose looked up at the woman's face. Recognition slowly dawned. It's was the lady with the sunny brown hair and out of the sun dark brown hair she'd caught Dad staring at earlier. The woman offered her a slight smile. No harm done, luckily. Her smile wavered. You nearly wore my dinner. I should have looked where I was going. Like I said, no harm done. Have a nice night. The lady circled around her and scanned the room, finally choosing a seat at an empty table in the far corner. Something better to do, huh? Rose thought about what she'd told Cherry maybe a new lady friend would keep her dad busy so Rose could enjoy her time at camp without being smothered. Besides, he needed someone in his life. They both needed someone. She'd overheart conversations between dad and gram, and knew her mother had been a big disappointment to him grams words, not his but maybe in a place like this Rose could find a woman who didn't think kids with new hearts were such a big deal. Maybe the light brown haired lady? She didn't have any kids with her. Uh oh, what are you thinkin? Cherry asked. I know that look good. It's good. I have a plan that's going to get us into trouble, look." Rose grinned. Yep, I have a plan. And you're going to help me. I think dad needs something better to do at camp than worry about me, and I think maybe a girlfriend is just what he needs. The two girls burst into giggles, then hooked their pinkies together. Best friends for life? Cherry asked. Best friends for life, Rose agreed. And then some." Nellie eased farther into the shadows, resting her back against a gnarled tree. A roaring bonfire and lit torches illuminated the man made beach along the lake. The chatter of families mingled with pops and crackkles as the fire shifted, the aroma of burning wood filled the air. Hi, again. The little girl from the dining hall held out a thin stick with something on the end. I brought you a toasted marshmallow to say I'm sorry for running into you. That was very thoughtful. Nellie pushed off the tree and bent over, trying to get a good peek in the dim light. Are you sure you don't want it yourself? The child lifted one shoulder. I've had my limit I made this one for you. Thank you. Nellie's fingers sank into the gooey peace offering, and she tugged it off the end of the stick, then popped it into her mouth. Mmm, delicious. Actually, it was a burnt cinder surrounding moltin goo, but she didn't want to hurt the child's feelings, she swallowed and forced a smile. I haven't had a toasted marshmallow in a long time. Thanks again. You're welcome. The little girl grinned. Where are your kid's? Nellie don't have any? Someday, maybe she'd figure out the right way to answer this question, a way that acknowledged Daniel but didn't reveal the depth of her pain. For now, she took the easy way. Don't you like kids? I'm a teacher. As if that guaranteen liking kids. The corner of the child's mouth spread further, Cool. Are you married? No, I'm not." She had to get this conversation back into safer territory. Are you? The little girl giggled. Not yet. She rolled her eyes heavenward. Probably never if my dad has his way. Speaking of dad she whipped her head around, pigtails flying I gotta go. Later." She scampered off into the crowd surrounding the bonfire. Cut kid. I wonder which of her siblings had a transplant? Nellie worked a cinder loose from a molar with her tongue and discreetly got rid of it. Why kids thought marshmallow had to go up in flames to be toasted was beyond her. But still, it had been a sweet gesture. It reminded her of the time Daniel decided to make breakfast f or her. Captain crunch cereal, orange juice and toast. That toast had launched her into laughter for weeks outside of Daniel's hearing, of course. Burned to the point of being something she could have used as a roof tile, the toast had peanut butter, jelly, honey and cream cheese poled on top of it her son's effort to cover up the black part. And she'd eaten every bite with a smile and done her best to keep it down. Kids the familiar ache began to build inside her chest, and she did her best to keep that down, too. Then some one blew into a microphone, intoning 'the standard testing, one two, followed by the mandatory taps on the head of the mike. Is this thing working? Yes! Several voices answered at once. Good, good, the man continued. Just in case I didn't get to greet you today, I'm Donald Brown. I run this camp with my wife, Trudy. The crowd broke into applause, and he held up a hand. Now, now, you might want to wait until the end of camp to see if you still feel like applauding me. We love ya, Don! Some one yelled. Camp firefly wishes is the best! Assed another youthful voice. Don chuckled and ran a hand over his scraggly beard. We like to think so. I want to welcome you all to camp, and officially open the session with the traditional lighting of the memory torch. A low hum passed through the crowd. People shuffled their feet in the sand. The hair on the back of Nellie's neck rose. Memory torch Memory torch? Trudy joined her husband on the sand near the small sound system. Painted stripes in the spectrum of the rainbow swirled down the handle of the white torch she carried. Don cleared his throat. Those of you who've been here before know this is our way of remembering those we've lost. Most of us know people who never made it off the transplant lists, people who died waiting. Trudy moved closer and laid a hand on her husband's shoulder.

The pair exchanged a glance so filled with support and a special bond that Nellie felt a sharp pang of envy. Loveing support from a spouse would be most welcome at this moment. Don reached up and patted his wife's hand before continuing. Our adult son was one of them. That's why we opened this camp. But this torch will burn brightly all while camp is in session, to remind us. We also want to dedicate it to the memory of those whose death gave others a second chance at life. This is for the donors and their families. Nellie stumbled backward until she bumped into the tree. She reached out and gripped the bark tightly between her fingers. As Trudy passed the torch to her husband and he lowered it to the flames of the bonfire, Nellie closed her eyes. She inhaled the cool night air deeply, then exhaled slowly. Without thinking, she pinched the bridge of her nose between her thumb and index finger to make the tingles go away a habit she'd developed since Daniels death. Whatever you're keeping locked inside you will eat you alive if you don't let it out. The deep, yet soft voice came from her side. Nellie opened her eyes and lowered her hand. Carlos.

I'm fine. Thanks for asking. He stood so close she smell his after shave, a rugged, masculine musk that went well with his chiseled facial features, blue jeans and shirt patterned in a Native American motif. You don't look like a psychologist. He smiled. And just what is a psychologist supposed to look like? Well, there are two schools of thought on that. One is the stuffy, suit wearing, tie and glasses psychologist who ran rats through mazes in college and now sits behind dest with a clipboard, murmuring Ah ha and I see. They like to run IQ tests and personaality profiles. And the other? The new age, beared, potbellied psychologist who burns incense. Looks like don over there. In college, instead of running rats through a maze, he set them free. He says things like and how does that make you feel? And what do you think about it? And you base these stereotypes on...? I work with a few of the first types at school. What about the second ones? I've run into a few of them, here and there. And none of the therapists she'd seen at other peoples urging had helped. None of them understood that she just wasn't ready. Marriage counseling? He stared entently at her mouth. You mentioned your ex earlier. Sort of. Music swelled in the background. Peering around his shoulder, Nellie could see Don and several other campers with guitars, glaring up for a singalong. Camp songs about poison ivy and missing meatballs and green speckled frogs, she could handle, but if they get sappy, she would simple leave. She turned back to Carlos and caught him still staring at her. What? Why are you looking at me like that? You've got something stuck on the corner of your mouth. He cupped her chin with one hand and ran the pad of his other thumb over the crease in her lips. What ever it is, its sticky. His hands were warm, touchin her lightly yet confidently, conveying quit stringh. Her mucles softened like the inside of that marshmallow. She chuckled, more from nerves at his touch than humor. That's my bunt offering. Burnt offering? He made another burnt offering? He made another pass with his fingers over her lips. I can't get it. Its going to need something more. Sorry. The hand cupping her chin vanished. She ran her tongue along the juncture of her lips several times, then used a fingernail to scrape at it. Did I get it? Uh, yeah, you got it. Thanks. Would't want to walk around with marshmallow on my face all right. Daddy! Carlos stiffened at rose's voice behind him. He backed away from Nellie and whirled to face his daughter. Yeah, tiger? I just wondered where you were, that's all. His cheeks grew warm, and quilt spread over him like refrigerated honey.

I'm sorry, Rose. I thought you were with Cherry and her family? But they're going back to their cabin. The baby's getting fussy, and her mom say's she's not feeding him in a crowd of people. Rose crande her neck to peek a round him. Who are you talking to? Just our neghbor. Yes we've kinda met, dad I bumped into her at dinner. Carlos looked from Nellie to his daughter. Bumped into her? Literally? Um, yes. Rose batted her lashes at him and grinned. No biggie, though. Right? Carlos sway his gaze back from child to woman. Woman. No biggie, though. Nellie shook her head. No biggie. She apologized. She edged away from the tree and around them. I have to

I have to get back to my cabin. Busy day tomorrow. He reached out and brusted his hand again her elbow. Elbow what's the rush? We'll walk walk back with you. Nellie leaned in closer to him, pitched her voice low. I thought you said your daughter had a heart transplant? I did, Rose piped up, obvously picking up the words not intended for her. Wanna see my scar? No! Nellie eyes widened, the moonlight illuminated a wildness in them. No, I don't she stumbled sideways, and when Carlos reached to steady her, she took off. Oops. Sorry dad. His daughters small hand slipped into his own, and she gave it a squeeze. He leaned over and planted a kiss on the top if her head. Its all right, unsinkable. Some people just don't do well with things like that. Like your mother. And obviosly his new neighbor. He tempered an unexpected surge of disappointment at the thought. I've warned you before about flashing that scar. I'm glad it doesn't bother you, but you have to be considerate about other peoples feelings. Beside, a little modesty would be a good thing. Its late allready, and tomorrow you have a lot of stuff going on. Okay dad. Rose picked at a piece of lint on the covers. Do you think that lady me now? No, of course not. I think you caught her by surprise, to him. That made twice she'd bolted when confronted with his daughters condition. How come you, don't go out on dates like other divorced parents? Whoa. How old are you now? Seventeen? I don't think my dating is really your business, tiger. But why don't you? Cherry's mom found Eddie, and now they're a real family. Aah, I see. Carlos leaned over and tapped gently on her nose. I don't date sweet heart because you are a very special girl, and I would have to find a very, special lady to be good enough for us. He brushed his lips over her forehead, ever vigilant of the temperture of her skin. I love you, unsinkable." She groaned. I love you, too, but I hate that name." I know. It's a fathers privilege to give his daughter a nickname she can't stand. Lights out in ten. The bed creaked again. He headed for his own room. A soft yellow glow illuminate the neighboring cabins. Nellie Bush he murmured. What's your story? His thought's wandered to the flicker of pal he'd seen in her eyes at their first meeting. There was obviously more to Nellie than she was prepared to reveal. Then the image of her walking away from him flashed into his consciousness. He didn't need a woman tempting him. Because this trip was for Rose. Her needs came first. As always. His needs...well his needs could wait. They'd waited this long. So he went to bed and got some sleep. They had breakfast, and later on a buzzer rang, announcing lunch time, and the kids scrambled from their chairs to swam the door where some parents already awaited them. Hey make sure everything is cleaned up before you go! Nellie shouted over the pandemonium before looking back to the doctor. She is find. The doctor gripped Nellie's hand and smiled at her. Good idea with the soap. I will remember this. A little earlier Nellie had helped Cherry get get out of a bad trap between two tables. Her left foot was caught and Nellie used soap to free the child. Come, Cherry, let us lit find your parents and get some ice for your foot. The doctor was refering to that trouble Cherry had gotten herself into earlier. Rose followed them as far as the back of the room, where she began to help clean up. Nellie sank onto the edge of the table and covered her face with trembling fingers, the adrenaline rush fading as her pulse throbbed in her skull. She inhaled deeply and slowly exhaled, trying to compose herself. A little excitement, huh? Nellie lowered hie hands to find Carlos standing nearby. Just a tad. In the back, Rose and several other children placed finished projects on the drying taable and tidied up the work areas with the help of some other parents. How do you do it? Do what? Live with the fear that you could lose her at any time? His eyebrows tightened and drew downward, and a scowl twisted his mouth. First of all, don't you ever, ever say anything like that within earshot of daughter." He glanced over his shoulder, then turned back to her. Second, don't shoot your mouth off when you have no clue what you're talking about. I'm...I'm sorry, I just –No excuse. Positive thinking, positive speaking, positive outcome. So please don't talk negatively around my kid. He turned and walked away. But I do have a clue. When she'd been a parent, she'd been oblivious to that kind of fear. Despite being concerned and safety minded, she'd never lived with the constant threat of losing her child. But now she knew all too well how quickly life could change. The crowded lunchroom hummed with the happy chatter of kids and parents along with the clink of utensils against dishes

Somewhere a baby wailed. Nellie lingered in the door way, debating going in. Her stomach hadn'd settled since the excitement of Cherry's ordeal, and the smell of grilled chicken and burgers did little to help. Miss Nellie Miss Nellie! A redheaded blur streaked in her direction from the other side of the room, arms waving madly. She glanced toward the door, contemplating a quick exit, when she noticed another red head gazing in her directions. Trudy brown was on the job, eyes trained directly on her from beneath a rainbow sweat band. Oop." Nellie exhaled sharply as Rose collided with her. The little girl wrapped her arms around Nellies middle and squeezed tightly. Thank you! You were so great! Nellie stiffened, muscles contracting. Trudy was still watching. Nellie patted Rose on the back several times, Not only was a hug from a child something she'd become uncomfortable with, but this ones father was still annoyed with her, judging by the scowl he sent her from a table in the far corner. And now Trudy was moving in her direction. Aah, summer camp. Toss in case of poison ivy and some stinging insects, and lofe didn't get much better than this. Your job depends on this she reminded herself. Jerry had been covering for her with the superintendent for a while now, and this was her last chance to make a good impression. She had to get a favorable report from the camp directors, had to prove she could get her act together. Come and eat with us, Miss Nellie, Rose invited, looking up at her. There's room at our table. Cherry is back from the doctors office and you can meet her parents. Thank you, Rose, but I don't" Trudy brushed past. I heard tell about your quick thinking earlier. Good job. And I think having lunch with this child is a wonderful idea. The woman pushed the sweatband higher on her forehead the multicolors clashing with her mane of hair. Perhaps camp firefly wishes is already working its magic on you? Nellie forced a smile and disentangled herself from Rose's embrace. Perhaps it is. She gave Rose's pony tail a gentle tug. I'll join you in a minute. The girls quick grin showed a missing side tooth, then she turned and skipped off, back toward her father. Trudy shook her head and tutted. It's sad, isn't it? What? A sweet little girl like that with no mama. The woman's hazel eyes followed the child's progress back to her table. And with such a handsome daddy. She looked at Nellie He's...easy enough on the eyes. Trudy's face lit up, and she patted Nellies shoulder before moving off; several minutes later, tray laden with a salad, bread and butter, and iced tea, Nellie approached the table, hoping no one could notice the trembling that made the tea in the glass rock from side to side. The only empty spot was next to Carlos. A petite brunnette woman rocked a fussing baby in her arms while the lanky blond haired man on the other side of Carlos stretched across the table, trying to pop a pacifier into the tiny mouth I hope–Rose invited me to join you." Carlos glanced up. The apprehension in Nellie's hazel brow eyes softened the tightness in his chest. Which irritated him all the more. He ground his teeth together, wanting to hold on to his anger with both hands to offset the temptation of wanting to hold on to her. When he'd seen her shaking after Cherry's mishap, gathering her into his arms had been an over whelming impulse. Until she'd made her little comment about the possibility of losing Rose at any time. He remided himself of how his ex used to say the same thing. Her tray rattled ominously as he continued to stare at her. Finally, he shifted along the bench. No sense in making a scene in front of everyone. Have a seat. Rose jumped to her feet. We're goin to get some dessert. We'll be back. Fruit, young lady, he reminded. No sweets. you ate enough marshmallows last night to equal that giant marshmallow guy in the gostbusters movies. Rose rolled her eyes at him. Funny, dad. Very funny not. The rest of the adults chuckled as the girls trotted off. The man on the other side of Carlos cleared his throat and raise his voice as the baby broke into long stretching screams. Aren't you going to introduce us, Carlos? He jerked his head in Nellie's direction. Yeah, sorry, Nellie bush, this is Eddie and Michelle Anderson Cherry's parents. It's a pleasure to meet you. That was good thinking using soap to get Cherry out of that table. Thank you. Michelle struggled to her feet. I'm sorry, but I've got to go feed Tyler before he breakse every ones eardrums. I'll come with you, honey. I'm sure Carlos will spare one eye for Cherry. Eddie leapt from the bench, pausing to lean over and whisper in Carlos ear, make sure Cherry gets to her next activity, will you, jimbo? This kids is due for a nap after his feeding, and then its a little r and r for mommy and daddy. Eddie straightened up and waggled his eyebrows, then winked at Carlos before escorting his wife from the room. I guess I sure know how to clear a table, don't I? Nellie murmured. Looks that way. The hazal brown eyes widened. She picked up her tray and rose to her feet. This was a mistake. Ill fine someplace else to sit. Just sit down and eat. You're already here, and there's not much lunch period left. He took her tray and set it back on the table. Not that there's much here for you to eat. No wonder you're so damn thin. You have a dgree in nutrition as well? I've become something of an expert in healthy diets.

Because of Rose? No, because my eighty–two–year old grand mother is in training for the iron man competition. Nellie paused in the middle of lifting a forkful of salad to her mouth shook her head. You're awfully sarcastie foe a psychologist. Or is it just me that brings out the worst in you? It's just you. It's just you. She set the fork back down. Look, Carlos, I'm really sorry I upset you earlier.

I certainly had no intention of doing so. I was coming down from a state of panic over Cherry, and I said the first thing that came to mine. He sighed the niggling image of her leaning against the tree last night, eyes shelt, breathing ragged, reminded him that this was a woman who was covering up some kind of pain. He didn't own the market on pain, and he shouldn't be acting like such a damn jackass, After all, she hadn't knowingly parroted Tiffany's words to him. He cleared his throat. I over reacted. Its just that I don't like Rose to hear any negative thoughts. Things are tough enough for her, I don't like to make matters worse. She doesn't seem like her health is uncertain. In fast, I have to confess, here. Nellie turned to eating. That's a wonderful thing to say to the parent of a transplant kid. Because if you could have seen most of them before their transplant, you'd never believe these are the same kids. Did Rose look different? If you don't mind me asking? Yeah, she did. Very much. He chugged the last few swallows of his pop to avoid saying anything else. A mental picture of his little girl, pale and too tired to play, taunted him. Was she always sick? I mean, what makes a child need a new heart? In her case, a congenital defect. She had a lot of carrective surgeries, but in the end, transplant was the only option. Nellie's face lost its color and she dropped her gaze to her plate. She pushed a cherry tomato around her salad bowl with her fork. Nellie? She briefly, met his gaze, then quickly looked down at her tray, but not before he'd seen a shimmering in her eyes. He reached out and getly clasped her hand. What is it? Sharing some times eases the burden. And I can assure you, I've pretty much heard it all in my practice. Dad! Guess what? Rose and Cherry skidded to a stop next to the table. Carlos yanked his hand back from Nellie's. Where did mom and Eddie go? Oh, man, I can't believe this, Cherry wailed. Why, what's wrong? Nellie asked. I signed them up for the adults three legged race, and now they're not here. There'll be prizes and everything! I'm sure they'll be disappointed, Nellie said hiding a small smile behind her butteredroll.

Yes, very, Carlos agreed solemnly. Although he was fairly certain Eddie had a different sort of sporting event in mind for him and his wife. A brief pang of envy rolled over him. But that's okay, Rose announced, because we've got more news. You do? Carlos eyed his daughter warily. What? I signed you up for the race, too. Rose! Who am I supposed to race with? The hazal eyes lit with glee. With Miss Nellie, of course. This is silly, this is silly, Carlos muttered as he tied their ankles together with a rag provided by the enthusiastic Trudy. He picked up another scrap of fabric and moved their knees, trying to keep his hands and mind from registering how soft her skin was and just how much of that skin was pressing against his. Mmm, Nellie hummed, in what he took to be her agreement. But your little girl looked so excited about the idea. Besides, its been a long time since I did any thing... fun Carlos glanced up in time to catch the fleeting expression of sorrow in her eyes. And why is that? He asked gently. Guess I just haven't been in a very fun mood lately. For any particular reason? She leaned over and tugged at the binding around their knees, effectively letting him know she didn't want to talk about it whatever it was. He divorce, maybe? He knew well enough how that experience could sour someone on fun for a long time. Too tight? he loosened the strip of cloth. How's that? This is great, Rose whispered to Cherry on Tuesday morning durning arts and crafts. I dunno, Rose. Neither one of them looked real happy when they found out yesterday. And did you notice that Miss Nellie kinda disappeared after that? Cherry reached across Rose and grabbed the glue bottle. She did not. She had to do arts and crafts with the little kids in the afternoon. I didn't see her at dinner or the night activaities, did you? No. Rose admitted, working a garn mane onto hir lion puppet. So how else are we gonna get my dad to notice her? Getting him to actually take her for that dinner would be good. I'll try. Tell him she'll be disappointed if he doesn't. Eddie hates it when mom is disappointed in him. Several tables over, Miss Nellie was helping another girl cut out a trunk for an elephant. Do you think he even likes her a little? she whispered. If her father didn't like Miss Nellie at all, then Rose would have to find another lady to distract him.

But there weren't too many women around without husbands. Besides, he'd already taken a liking to Miss Nellie. Cherry laughed. Didn't you see the way he was looking at her yesterday, Shh! Here she comes. Rose smiled as Miss Nellie approached their table. How's it going girls? I trust noones is getting stuck today? Nope, Rose responded. Will you have lunch with us again? Oh, I don't know. I have to —Miss Nellie your purse is ringing? Sean yelled. Nellie glanced over her shoulder. Thank you. She smiled tentatively at Carlos daughter. I'll have to get back to you. Saved by the bell. Then wagged a finger. Jamie, get those scissors away from your hair and back on the project where they belong, you're way too old for that kind of nonsense. This is not beauty school. Sound's like you're busy, Nellie. I'll call back later. I had a meeting with the superintendent this morning. He was very interested in how you're doing at the camp. Wanted to know if you were making progress, dealing with things Jerry cleared his throat, uh, emotional issues, as he called them. Nellie left the art room, leaning against the walls just outside the door for support. Emotional issues! Her son had died, and the superintendent was talking about emotional issues. Hell yeah, it was an emotional issue! And you told him? I told him you were working on it, Nellie. Jerry's voice softened. How is it going, champ? Its going...great, Jer. How did he think it was going? She was surrounded by kids whose lives had been saved by transplants. Kids who'd survived. While hers...hadn't. Don't pull thata with me. I'm just worried about you, that's all. Nellie pinched the bridge of her nose. She peesed at her students, through the square window in the door, making sure they were doin what they should be, that no one was trapped in a chair or cuting their hair. I know, Jerry. And I appreciate it. I just don't know that you can order this kind of healing, although I know my dad likes to think he can. He chuckled gruffly. If anybody could order it, it could be the sarge. But he's as concerned about you as I am, don't mistake it. I know, in fact, lots of people are concerned about you. Peter called me this morning. The muscles along her neck knotted, and she growled into the phone. What's the rule about mentioning that man's name? She didn't care if Peter was Jerry's only newphew, he knew where she stood on hearing about him. You send me to this camp, call me up to tell me the superintendent is still concerned about my fitness in the classroom, and then you throw Peter at me? What's next? Along sigh floated from the phone receiver. I hate being caught between the two of you. You know I love you as if you were my own daughter but Peter is my blood. I hate the hurt he's put you through, but I can't turn my back on him any more than I can you, through your father would sure be happy if I washed my hands of Peter. I'm not asking you to. Just don't talk to me about him. And don't talk to him about me. He's out of my life now, and that's that. There wasn't anything left to connect them, not even their child. Though they'd been separated for several months before the accident she'd only taken back her maiden name when the divorse became final. She wanted no link to the man she held responsible for her babys death. She shook I think my batterys going dead, Jer. I'll call you later in the week. Flipping the phone closed, she returned to the room, the chatter of the kids washing over her. The scents of glue and paper, of drying wild flowers picked by the group of five to seven year olds the preuious afternoon, stirred feelings of loss and longing within her. If she wasn't a mother anymore, and the superintendent removed her from the classroom so that she was no longer a teacher, then what was she nothing. Other parents were unfolding chairs, arranging them in a circle in the shade of the gently swaying oaks. Eddie trudged across the lawn, chair is in either hand. Michelle followed with Tyler in a front carrier. She waved to Carlos, and he returned the gesture. Nellie stood off to the side of the group, biting her lower lip and scanning the crowd. Her rigid posture spoke volumes on the subject of her discomfort. Carlos had taken a step in her direction before he'd even realized it, only to be stopped by Don's hand on his arm. Don't. Do me a favor don't sit anywhere near her, the impression I've gotten of her is she's not going to open up if anyone gets too close. And beleive me, that young woman needs to open up. I know that. In fact, I pracally told her so the first night of camp. You did? And how did she respond? She ignored it. Changede the subject. Carlos reviewed her behavior durning their conversation, and then realized that she was about to join a group for transplant parents. Oh groaned softly. Oh, don't tell me. He stared hard at Don. Did she lose a transplant child? That's for her to tell, if she chooses. You should know better than to ask me. This camp is a place for healing, a place for everybody to deal with their transplant experiences. Why do you think we include the whole family? Carlos wanted Nellie hesitantly open her chair and position it slightly back from the others. I don't know, I figured it made it easier for the kids. No, its because everyone in the family is affected by having a sick child, including the brothers and sisters. And because we wanted to give parents a place where they can just be people again. A place where they could just be people again? Carlos wasn't sure he knew how to be just a man anymore. He'd been the single father of a medically needy kid for so long now that he'd almost forgotten what it was like to deal with his own needs, his own desires. Don clapped his hands. Okay, folks, let's get settled so we can start. Carlos positioned himself beside Don so he could watch Nellie on the farside of the circle. This afternoon she wore a white shirt with patriotic read, white and blue stars across the neckline. The camp director opened the session by saying they could discuss anything, whether it related to transplants, child, rearing whatever they wanted. An awkward stillness fell over the group before someone began to talk. Topics ranged from dealing with sibling rivalry to medications. Eddie brough up the unique trials and joys of step parenting a transplant child. His love for Cherry shone clearly in his face as he spoke, and Carlos found himself happy for Michelle, glad that someone had found a mate who could handle the demands of a sick child. And Eddie had been there, as much as possible, through the whole thing. He and Michelle had started dating about six months before Cherry's heart transplant. They'd married soon afterward. Carlos and Rose hadn't made it to the wedding because Rose had still been in the hospital. You know something I'm curious about, Don said durning a conversation. How many of you have had contact of any kind with your donor families? Nellie straightened in her chair so fast she almost fell out of it. I am the donor, one mom said, and I've got the scars to prove it. She rubbed her stomach while others chuekled knowingly. Part ofc of envied her. How wonderful it would have been to be able to give Rose what she needed himself. Unfortunately people did't come with spare hearts. Kidneys livers even lung transplants were being done with living donors, but hearts...they were beyond living donor capabilities. That's fantastic, I'm sure it was a great relief for you to be able to donate your kidney to Sean. But I wasn't talking about living donors, whom you often know before the surgery. Don scanned the circle of parents. Anybody here have an experience with an unrelated, unknown living donor? Heads shook all around the group. So what about the rest of you? Nellie gasped, then pressed her hand over her mouth, eyes going wide. Nellie? Was there something you wanted to say? Don asked. She shook her head slowly, lowering her hand back down into her lap. No. Nellie murmured something that had the neighboring woman glaring at her. Carlos leaned forward in his chair. What was that, Nellie? I didn't hear you. She lifted her chin and met his gaze. I said, maybe they weren't ready. Nobody seems to understand that sometimes people just aren't ready. Aren't ready for what? Nellie? Don asked gently. To face it, to deal with it...She lifted both shoulders and let them fall again. The woman next to her shifted to face her head on. Look, no no offense...Nellie, is it? Nellie nodded. I'm just not sure what your credentials are to be part of this discussion. I mean, I know you're teaching arts and crafts to two of the kids groups, but other than that, why are you here? Nellie looked stricken by the woman's words, and as much as he wanted to know the answer to that particular question, too, Carlos couldn't help but wanted to throttle the tactless lady. Come on girl, tell them, Don murmured under his breath. Lay your cards on the table. Carlos shot him a sharp glance, then returned his attention back to Nellie she had her thumb at her mouth and was chewing on the nail, eyes cast downward at the grass in front of her chair.

Well? The busybody in the next chair folded her arms imperiously across her chest, the queen waiting for a response. His stomach constricted when Nellie briefly looked at him. Not close enough to see for certain, he could guess that there were unshed tears in her eyes. He started to rise, but Don's befy hand clamped over his forearm. Don't. Sit still and hope she pops, Don said softly. Credentials? Nellie asked in a tremulous voice you want my credentials? She turned and glared at the other woman. A pair of lungs, two kidneys, a liver and a heart. How's that for credentials? I–I don't understand, said her majesty. Nellie jumped to her feet, knocking over her lawn chair. Dammit, why doesn't anyone care that I'm not ready for this? She yelled. Visible tremors shook her entire body as she let her gaze slip from person to person around the circle. My only child, Daniel, my baby, was a donor. Carlos slid to the edge of his seat, heart in his throat at her revelation. Oh, Nellie. Stunned silence descended upon the group until the only sounds were the chirping birds in the shade providing trees. She slapped a hand over her mouth as though realizing what she'd just said, and turned her back on the circle. The woman on the other side of her rose to drape an arm around Nellie's shoulder. Nellie whirled, nearly tripping on the over turned chair, and stumbled into the center of the group. Don't don't touch me. Tell us about Daniel, Nellie, Don encouraged. Tell us about Daniel, your son. We want to hear about him. He looked to the parents for support. Right? Murmur of agreement floated up from all around the circle. She shook her head. No I can't...You can. A solitary tear tracked slowly down her right cheek. Carlos heart shattered into a thousand tiny pieces for her. It was one thing to live with the fear of losing your child quite another to deal with the reality of it. I have to go, she announced, pinching the top of her nose briefly. I have to go. She squared her shoulders and lifted her chin, striding quickly toward an opening in the circle. Once she passed the ring of chairs, the facade of decorum vanished. She broke into a trot, then a flat out run in the direction of the cabins. Carlos jumped to his feet, only to be stopped once more by Don's grip on his arm. Let go of me, he said firmly. This time I'm going to her. She needs someone. She does. See if you can get her her to talk. MAKE HER TELL YOU ABOUT HIM. The older psychologist released him. Carlos raced after her, catching a fleeting glimpse of denim and long legs as she dashed around the corner of the main building as though pursued by the devil himself. Nellie's feet pounded the dirt road as she hurtled toward her cabin, desperately controlled tears blurring her vision. Her stomach churned, and her heart, her heart arched with an intensity she hadn't thought possible anymore. The screen door to the porch slammed shut behind her as she bursst through the cabin entry..just inside, she crumpled into a heap, the harsh green carpeting burning her bare skin. She rolled onto her side, knees drawn up; and gave the tears free rein. Oh, Daniel, she sobbed. She breathed in jerking gasps, exhaling on a sob. Her nose ran, and tears trickled down into her open mouth carrying the faint taste of salt. On the edge of her consciousness she heard the screen door slam, but was too deep into her grief to worry about who was going to find her in this pathetic condition. Her marriage was over, her son was gone, her career threatened. What did it matter anymore? Nellie, a deep voice murmured. Warm hands circled her back. That's it, you let it go. Strong arms gathered and lifted her, carried her to another place. Soothing words washed over the edge of her brain. She buried her face into Carlos firm chest and sobbed as though her world had ended. Time ceased to have meaning. She'd never known such pain. Or paradoxically, such comfort. Carlos held her close and rocked her, his warmth and motion a soothing balm on her raw soul. He stroked her hair, crooned words of encouragement as she continued to flood his shirt with her her tears. When at last she had the strength to lift her head from his chest and look at him, the compassion and empathy in his eyes nearly broke her composure again. He cupped her cheek in his palm, brushing her final tears away with his thumb. Better? She nodded, but then lifted her shoulders in a shrug. Tired. I'm sorry about your son, Nellie. The image of his face blurred and she swallowed hard. Thank you. She whippered. Will you tell me about him? I–I need a tissue. She sniffed to illustrate her point. Oh, look at your shirt. He glanced down at the trails of moisture, then smiled at her. It'll wash. She tried to force an answering smile for him. God knew, he deserved it cradled in his arms, she felt safe, protected, comforted. No one had everhelped her like this and allowed her to weep all over them, not Peter certainly not her father. Anew sence of loss washed over her when he gently lifted her from his lap and set her in the corner of the sofa. He climbed to his feet. Don't go! She reached for his hand. I'm not. He squeezed her finger reassuringly. I'm just going to get you that tissue. What a mess she'd made of things, not counting his shirt. Now they all knew about Daniel. She'd broken down in front of a group of strangers. How would she face them again? Carlos returned from the bathroom with a box of tissues and a warm, wet wash cloth. Here, wipe your face. It'll make you feel better. Not to mention look better, I probably have mascara tracks down my face and look like hell, don't I? That's one of those questions a sane man know's not to answer. He took the wash cloth back from her. Here, let me. He knelt in front of her, then swiped the clothe across her cheeks. There. He tossed the wet terry cloth onto the glass end table. Carlos lowered himself to the sofa at her side. Now, you were going to tell me about your son. I was? Yes you were. Are trying to counsel me? Do you think you need a counselor? She condidered it for a moment. Maybe it was time. Probably. But...I think I need a friend more. Something ominous like a thunderhead, crossed his expression, darkening his face for the slightest moment before he inhaled deeply and sighed. She averted her eyes. I'm sorry. That was rather presumptuous of me. No! His fingers cupped her chin and lifted it until their gazes met. I'd like that very much, Nellie. His thumb grayed the underside of her lower lip, setting off sparks deep in her belly. The weight of his gaze on her mouth birthed the irrational hope that he would kiss her. Maybe the pain would go away. On at least be forgotten for a moment.

I want...Won't what? I want– he lowered his hand to help her. She smothered her hand disappointment and shifted on the sofa, tucking her feet beneath her legs. She yanked the sunflower pillow from behind her back and clutched it in her lap. Of course he didn't want to kiss her, she looked a fright and she'd collapsed like a bobbling baby in his presence. Her cheeks tingled as she studied a piece of lint stuck to the black center of the pillow. Will you let me help? She nodded. Then tell me about Daniel, he urged softly. How he died? She hadn't been there at the time of the accident on the play ground. It had been Peter's weekend with Daniel, but she'd pictured the scene enough times in her mind, still, she didn't know if she could actually talk about it. First tell me how he lived. Warmth flooded Nellie's chest as she allowed the memories of Daniel to escape their hiding place. A tiny smile tugged at her lips. Always on the move. Daniel was all boy I swear, the only time he relaxed was when he was asleep. Must have been hard to keep up with him. There were days when I fell asleep about ten minutes after he did. Carlos groped for the right words, the words that would help her see how much her bravery in Daniel's death had meant to others. Rose was rarely like that before the transplant. Infact, there were days when all she did was sleep. Her body just didn't have the strength for being a regular kid. Poor thing. Nellie murmured. She has so much zip now. Exactly. And that's because someone out there had the courage, just like you. To donate a beloved heart so my little girl could live, and have a chance to be a kid. He leaned forward and took her hand. Nellie, what you did was a wonderfully brave and unselfish thing. You and Daniel are heroes. You saved lives. An ember of the fire appeared in her hazel brown eyes. I wasn't being brave and unselfish, only logical. And you know what? The only life I wanted to save, I couldn't. I understand. I felt helpless with Rose, too. You don't understand. She yanked her hand free and jumped from the couch, hurling the pillow into the corner she'd vacated. Your child lived! Mine didn't. Why? Do you ever ask yourself that? I do. He rose to his feet but kept his distance from her. The hardest thing about being a transplant parent is sitting at your child's bed, praying for a miracle is the death of someone else's child. They paced the small living room in parallel.

I really am sorry about Daniel, Nellie. You want to know the hardest thing about being a donor parent? Hell no! He had enough guilt over the whole thing without knowing. But she needed to tell him. Yes. The hardest thing for me was letting him go when he still had a beating heart. I knew in my head he was gone already, but my own heart, just couldn't seem to accept it. He was gone. But he didn't look gone. My dad took me to the chapel, and then they took Daniel away. I kept picturing him in a cold operating room table, surrounded by doctors and nurses who didn't know him, who didn't love him. Tears trickled slowly down her cheeks again. Oh, he'd been declared dead before that, but they needed to keep his heart beating. So it could be transplanted into some one like Rose. Though grateful for Nellie's and all the others like her courage, he would have proferred to live the rest of his life without the image of her small son on the operating table while she wrestled with her grief in a lonely hospital chapel. The image of her little boy still haunted him several hours later as he sat before a roaring campfire behind his cabin. Eddie and the girls were out on the road in front, catching lighting bugs in plastic cups, and Tyler slept in a baby seat behind his mothers chair. Moonlight flickered through the trees and frogs honked in a throuty chorus down near the lake. Do you even think about it Michelle? Carlo asked, leaning forward in the webbed lawn chair, prodding the bonfire ember with a long stick. I wondered when you were going to talk, she said. Think about what, exactly? The donors. Their families. Every day. So do I. But not like I did today. Carlos stirred the red coals. Usually I just think about how wonderful it was for them to help someone else in a time of tragedy. And I'm grateful. It was for them to help someone else. And I hope they've found peace. With their loss. But today...The frogs broke into another throaty refrain, and faint laughter rifted from the front of the cabin, filling the hole in the conversation. Today you ran smack into another parents grief and it scared the hell out of you. The stick slipped from his hand and dropped into the dirt at his feet. I can't wait to see your bill for this session, he murmured, bending over to retrieve it. You know, I don't practice cosmetology. And you shouldn't dabble in psychology. Ha! Shows what you know. In my neck of the woods in North Carolina, a beautician is a woman's soundin board, just like the bartender is for the men. And here I thought all you women did in a beauty salon was gossip. Carlos...Michelle folded her arms across her chest. You can't fool me. Probably not they'd spent a lot of time together in the hospital when both girls were waiting for heart's. Many cups of lousy coffee and late night chats had led to a valuable friendship. He'd rejoiced with her when Cherry had gotten her heart, and held her when she'd cried over her daughters early bout a rejection. But that didn't mean he wanted to hear her analysis of him. He glanced over at the next cabin. No lights burned inside. And he could imagine Nellie sitting in the dark, alone, trying to deal with the emotions they'd stirred up earlier. She didn't come to dinner. Maybe I should go and check on her. He cracked the stick in half over his knee and tossed the pieces into the fire, then rose to his feet. Michelle reached for his hand as he passed. Are you sure that's a good idea? She's dealing with this alone. No matter how bad things got for us, we were never alone. We had a support network at the hospital. I had my parents, you had Eddie. Who does she have? You're supposed to be here for Rose and you, not someone else. On vacation, remember? No pshchonalijzing? She needs a friend, Michelle. Just like we both did at children's hospital. But do you need a friend with that much baggage? We've all got baggage, but some peoples is heavier than others. He gave Michelle's hand a quick squeeze and released it. I'll be back in a few minutes. Let Rose know if she comes looking for me. Okay? She sighed. All right. But I'm telling you, this is a mistake. Was it? He pondered while he trudged toward Nellie's cabin. As a psychologist, he knew he could be of assistance. As father of a transplant kid, he felt a sense of obligation. He might never meet Rose's donor family, but he could express his gratitude to this surrogate. As a man...That was where he got into trouble. The memory of her soft curves pressed tightly against him as he cradled her in his arms provoked a flash of heat. Maybe Michelle was right. Maybe this was a mistake. Dad! Dad! Look! Carlos turned. Rose hurtled in his direction, white T shirt easily discernible in the moonlit night. Don't run in the dark! You'll fall. And dint roll your eyes at me. Her laughter as she slowed to a trot confirmed what he hadn't seen, but had guessed correctly. Look she shoved a plastic cup covered with cling wrap into his hands. I caught four lightning bugs. He lowered himself to one knee and studied her offering. The tiny creatures flickered yellow neon pulse from their tails. Aren't they cool? They sure are. Are you going to keep them in here? Nah, we'll let them go in a bit. Did you know you can make a wish when you set them free; and if they light up, your wish will come true? No, I didn't. Who told you that? Trudy and Don. That's why they named the Camp Firefly Wishes. He grabbed the end of her ponytail and gave it a gentle tug. And what will you wish for, Unsinkable? Da–ad. She groaned. First, I'll wish for you to stop calling me that. Then she grinned at him. And I'm not telling you what else, its a secret. Okay. Carlos handed his daughter the bug container. Rose glanced over his shoulder at the near by cabin. Are you going to Miss Nellie's just for a few minutes. I want to check on her. She had kind of a rough afternoon. Rose nodded. I know. I heard about her little boy. He gripped her shoulder. How did you hear about that? Its all over camp, Dad, Everyone is talking about it. Carlos sighed. He did his best to shelter her from stories like that, but she'd seen far more death than any eight year old should have. Here. Rose pressed the cup back into his hand. Maybe these will help. She probably needs some wishes. Don't you want them? I'll catch more. There's a bunch of them over in the bushes on the other side of the road. That's very sweet, tiger. You go ahead, because it's almost that time. Rose groaned, Don't I get to stay up later? It's camp! Its already past your usual bed time and you need your rest. He gave her a quick hug. Go on. All right. She scampered off in the direction of their cabin. Don't run! He shook his head kids. They never listened to words of warning. But then, sometimes neither did their father. The weathered boards of Nellie's porch step creaked beneath his feet, and the screen doors hinges squeaked. He paused outside the main entrance, tilted his head and listened. Nothing. She didn't respond to his rapping, either, so he cracked open the door and took a cautious step inside Nellie? It's me, Carlos. Silence, broken only by the rattle of the ceiling fan in her living room. His stomach tightened as her words of the afternoon came back to him. Dammit, doesn't anyone care that I'm not ready for this? Had they pushed her to far, too fast? Nellie? He checked the bathroom first, and loudly exhaled his relief upon not finding her there. Too many possibilities for doing harm to oneself in a bathroom. The bedroom door stood slightly ajar, and he swung it open, his relief complete. She sat cross legged in the middle of the bed, clutching a pillow in her arms. He flipped the light switch. She flinched, blinke hard against the sudden brightness, then swiveled until her baack faced him. Clothes littered the room. Khaki shorts and pastel shirts were draped across the open suit case on the luggage stand jeans cluttered the nearby floor. The dresser drawers hung at odd angles, most of them empty, one in the apparent process of being emptied. You going somewhere? He leaned against the door jamb and shoveed his right hand in his pocket, the left clutched Rose's lightning bugs. I thought about it. I didn't take you for a coward, Nellie running won't make the pain go away. The bugs flickered in their make shift holding cell, iridescent yellow flashes of hope. I'd wish it away for you, if I could. What will? Faceing it is a good start. Time will help. How long, Carlos? How long will it take to fill the hole in my heart? He didn't dare tell her there'd always be a hole, though smaller than than the one now threatening to consume her. I don't know. How long has it been since Daniel died? She rose off the farside of the bed and tossed the pillow at the headboard. Heading on a year and a half. She rubbed her temples. Or maybe its been forever. Sometimes I get confused. With an empty chuckle, she crossed to the suitcase, retrieved a turqoise blouse and began to fold it. They sent me for tests, you know. Who's they? My father. Jerry. The people who love me. Tests? Now he was the confused one. Yeah. Because of the forgetfulness. They did a CAT scan, an MRI, an EEG. Alphabet soup of tests. They thought something was wrong because I was never like that before. The shirt landed in the dresser drawer and she picked up another. Ofcourse something was wrong! My son was dead. He set the plastic cup on her night table and moved closer. Didn't anyone treat you for depression, Nellie? She snorted. Shows what you know doc bushes don't get depressed. They don't take pills in bad times. They lace their combat boots lighter and carry on like good soliers do. No one had to know. Just you. And not all treatments means pills. Alemony smelling shirt wrapped itself around his face, and he clawed at it. Make yourself useful and fold that. She strightened the dresser drawer. I live in a very small town, Carlos. Everyone knows everyone, and their business. The doc wouldn't blab, and probably not the pharmacist, but the big mouthed women who work in the drug store are another matter entirely. Why, they're so bad, practically nobody buys birth control in town. This time her laugh had a genuine hint of humor in it. The condoms there have a longer shelf life than spam. Carlos stepped closer to her, offering the folded garment. That's usually not a good thing. Tell me about it. The half smile she gave him faltered, and her lower lip quivered slightly. That's how I got Daniel. He put on his best nonjudgemental face, one he'd had a lot of practice with in his office. So, Daniel was a surprise! A delightful, wonderful surprise. The final piece of clothing vanished into the dresser and she slammed the drawer shut, then turned to face him. Why am I telling you this? Because I'm your friend. We established that this afternoon, remember? I have other friends, Carlos I don't talk to them about this. And that's your problem. Which I told you the first night. You can't hold all that stuff inside you without something happening. Like forgetfulness. Or ulcers. Or a bunch of other stress related illresses. Thank you, doctor sunshine. Her hazel brown eyes pleaded for something from him. Reassurance? I have something for you. You do? Yeah. Actually, it's from Rose. Come outside with me and I'll give it to you. He retrieved the plastic cup from the right table and cradled it in his hands, hiding it from her view. He left the bedroom and headed for the front of the cabin. What is it? She asked from behind him. Hey, at least give me a hint. No hints. He flipped on the porch light as he passed the switch, then led her out the screened door and down the steps okay, close your eyes. He waited a moment are they closed? I don't think I know you well enough to close my eyes. For crying out loud, Nellie just do it. Okay, okay. They're closed. He turned to her. Moonlight flickered softly over the gentle features of her upturned face. Her delicately shaped lips were slightly parted. Moonlight, closed eyes. Parted lips...God help him, she looked for all the world like a woman waiting to be kissed. Suddenly the need to kiss him ignited and burned like a wildfire in a drought scorched forest. He struggled to subdue the impulse a kiss was the last thing either of them needed. Well? She prompted. He cleared his throat. Uh, here. He closed her hands around the cup. You can open your eyes now. As if on cue, two of the tiny creatures flashed in unison. Oh, fireflies. Her voice caught. Daniel always loved catching fireflies in the summer. Trudy told the girls that if you make a wish and the fireflies flash when you release them, your wish will come true. She glanced back up at him and once more a solitary tear tracked down her cheek. His final shred of professionalism slipped away, and suddenly, he was just a man. He longed to gather her in his arms and soothe away all her pain. But Daniel didn't live long enough to lose a tooth, and mommy wasn't able to kiss it and make it better. I know. And a kiss from Carlos wouldn't make anything better for her, but dammit, he was tempted to try. And so you've stopped believing in magic. Haven't you? After all that Rose's been through, do you still believe in magic, Carlos? I still believe in miracles. That there's healing in laughter, and in the kindness of strangers. I believe in angels like you... and like Daniel. And what about firefly wishes? Do you believe in them? She held the cup closer to his face. Between the flickering insects and the dappled moonlight breaking through the swaying trees, he could see her eyes. He saw a tiny spark of hope, and he just couldn't crush it, any more than he could crush Rose's faith in magic. He reached for that unwavering faith of childhood that he'd tryed to instill in his daughter, the knowledge that all things were possible. The unsinkable Rose. She'd survived against the odds. Yes, he whispered. I believe in firefly wishes. And in that moment, he did. Good. Then wish with me, Carlos. There are four fireflies. Two apiece. But Rose wanted you to have them. You believe more than I do. And I'm sure she won't mind if I share them with her dad. She offered him a quivering smile. Your daughter is kind and loving, Carlos. You should be proud of her. I am. Nellie removed the elastic band from the cups rim, and lifted the plastic wrap. Ready? He nodded. Okay. Barries removed, the tiny insects crawled to the lip of the cup. The first one flitted into the air and hovered near their heads. That's yours! Wish Carlos! I wish healing for your aching heart, Nellie as it flew off, the bugs tail light flashed in farewell, and a gentle warmth flooded him. You got it. Here go the rest, get ready. She closed her eyes as the trio launched them selves off the cup. He held his breath, she scrunched her face tighten with the effort of wishing. He quickly glanced upward. Only one of them flashed Nellie blinked rapidly. Blast, I missed them. Did they flash? Yeah. Yeah, they did. A small lie, but then, it was the believing that was important, right? The power of positive thinking? God. The relief on her face made him curious. What did you wish for? I figureed unselfish wishes were best, so I wished for other people. You did?

Who? Isn't there a rule that says if you tell, then it doesn't come true? Not that I know of. My first wish was for you and Rose. Oh? Yes I wished Rose's new heart will stay strong and healthy so. You never know this pain. His own heart skipped a beat, then tried to crowl into his throat, the hair on the back of his neck prickled. How the hell did he respond to that? Shen'd meast well, but, damn, talk about hitting where it hurt. He cleared his throat. Thanks. No, parent should ever know the pain of losing a chid. No, she whispered. It's just not right. You never expect it. What was your second wish? He asked, seeing the clouds gathering in her eyes again. That the parents of Rose's donor would know peace in their loss. That's a very good wish, one that I make frequently. He captured her empty hand and gave it a little squeeze. One I wish for you. Too, Nellie. She lowered her head. Maybe one day. Not maybe one day you will. It will get easier, I promise. You you. Might not know it, but you made big strides toward that today. And how am I suppose to face those people tomorrow? That's why I was packing. I couldn't stand the idea of them looking at me and knowing, feeling sorry for me. Hey. He released her hand and lifted her chin with the tip of his index finger until she met his gaze. Pity and empathy are two different things. You've faced these parents greatest night mare. What did you wish Carlos? Me? Not about to confess his first, and having forgotten to make a second, he cast about for something to lighten the mood, something to distract her. I wished...He skimmed the underside of her bottom lip with his thumb, I wished for a kiss. Her eyes widened. She drew back her head, but he didn't release her. You did not. Did so. Or might have, anyway, had he thought about it. He traced them— shape of her upper lip, delighting in the selky texture beneath his fingertip. I very much want to kiss you, Nellie. Her mouth quivered under his fingers and she shook her head ever so slightly. I don't think that's a good idea. Probably not, but right now I don't really care. She slipped her palm to his chest and pushed. He dropped his hands from her face and sighed, Struggling to control the urge to dip his head and taste her. Okay. Then how about breakfast with Rose and me in the morning. Un.I...you have to eat. Instinct told him her thinness had a lot to do with the emotional baggage she carried, vanity. How many meals has she missed over the past year and a half? You might as well do it with us. Maybe She pressed the emty plastic cup into his hand. Give this to Rose so she can catch more fireflies if she wants. And tell her I said thanks for the wishes. She turned away from him and started up the creaky steps to her cabin. Nellie? She paused, glancing over her shoulder. Yes? There's no time limit in when firefly wishes come true I believe I'm going to get mine. Eventually, He winked at her. The tiny, halfhurted smile she gave him in returned made it all worthwhile. Maybe. Goodnight. Carlos. Shh. Rose pressed Cherry back into the bushes across the dirt road from Miss Nellie's cabin. Here he comes. The girls crouched among the branches. Hiding as her dad walked by. He had a weird expression on his face, one she'd never seen before. His eyes seemed I wider than normal. Then he shook his head, and his lips tighten into a thin line, like he did sometimes when he wasn't happy, with her. Rose covered her mouth with her hand and held her breath until he'd passed. Then she exhaled softly. Did you see that? Cherry whispered. He was going to kiss her. Really? Do you think so? Rose stood up and danced in place; causeing the shrub leaves to rustle. That's great. Its working. My plan is working! We need to keep them together somehow. Hey, if they go on that date, maybe I can stay with you while there gone. Maybe dad will even let me sleepover in your cabin. Wouldn't that be neat? I've never gone on a sleepover. We'll just have to get them together. And soon, all he'll be thinking about is Miss Nellie cool. And maybe then he'll forget about stopping me from having fun. Early morning sunbeams danced through the leaves, and birds chirped as Nellie strolled next day back up the overgrown path from the Mist Lake. She kicked arock and sent it skittering into the weeds. Sleep hadn't come easily the night before, and while she wanted to believe that the majority of her thoughts had been about Daniel and the the transplant children she'd met she had to admit Carlos had taken up way too many of them far more than his share. Far more than was wise. Finally there had been the dream. With Carlos. And the fireflys. And...Kissing. Lots of kissing. Heart pounding, toe curling, bone melting kissin. Kissing that led to more. Much more...She shook her head to throw off the lingering effects of the dream, the wonderful jumpy feeling that lodged in the warmth of her stomach. The reality was that after kissing came Sex, which led to susprise pregnancies and unplaned marriage, which resulted in wandering husband, and separations, fathers distraacted by their bimbos. Her throat tighened. And terrible accidents. She swallowed hard. She could be forgiven being scramble brained under the influence of moonlight, fireflies and caramel colored eyes filled with compasstion, but in the broad daylight, Nellie would allow herself no such leeway. She rounded the corner of the cabin and came face to face with the goat, which only served to rein force, the idea that kissing led to trouble. Coated in dust from the dirt roads, the car bore only a passing resemblance to the proud, clean, shiny toy that had spent most of its time in the garage. The bushes rustled and a tiny red squirrel das out streaked across the road and clambered onto the hood of the GTO. He posed there, a natural hood ornament, whiskers twitching as he rubbed his face with his little paws. Peter would have had a fit. What would Carlos say? The thought appeared from no where, but she considered it. He seemed to appreciate goat almost as much as Peter had. He occasionally even exuded the same smooth self confidence her Ex had. But last night, Peter would have belittled her hesitation and kissed her, anyway. Where Carlos had actually responed to her cues and not pushed. Which made him all the more attractive. The squirrel darted off the car as Nellie stomped her heel into the dirt. Troubler nothing but trouble. What's trouble? Don ambled up the dirt road, strings from his ragged denin cutoffs swinging against his thighs. She sighed. Given my life, the correct question is what's not trouble? He halted in his tracks, eyesbrows creeping toward his shaggy salt and pepper hair. He nodded at her, one hand caressing his beard. Wow. That was actually an open, honest acknowledgment of the fact that your life isn't what you want it to be. Good for you. Oh, Next thing, you'll be asking me how I feel about that. How do you feel this morning? Just fine and dandy, Thaks for asking. Don shook his head. There goes our honesty. People don't want honest, Don, they want comfortable. And guess what? People aren't comforable when you start blathering on about how rotten your life is, or that your son died and left behind a big hole and you're not quite sure how you're going to make it through another day. When people ask you how you are, they want you to say fine, I know about son size holes in your life. And I know you're not fine. She studied the chipped pink nail polish on her big toe, then lightly scuffed the dirt with the front of her sandal. Nellie glanced back at him. My son was twenty three when he died. He left behind a wife and a two year old daughter. I've been in the place where you are. He paused and ran his hand over his beard again. But life is about livin, and you need to move on. Figure out how best to honor Daniel's memory. By not letting life pass you by? Or by grabbing hold of it and squeezing out all you can? I'm trying to carry on. Like the good soldier I am. Dad should be proud. She pinched the bridge of her nose. You need to do more than carry on, Nellie. But it's a start. A good start. He offered her a pensive smile. I'm here to help. Do you have any questions for me? Oh, tons. Great. His smile widened. Like what? Like what do you do with this place for the other fifty weeks of the year? Nellie swept her arms in an expansive gesture to indicate the camp. Don chuckled. Okay, change the subject. That's fine. In the summer, we run a number of other programs, not just for transplant kids, although that's our pet project, obviously. We also run programs for aids kids, cancer kids and diabetic kids. Then, we do other things scout groups, family reunions, even corporate retreats. And Trudy and I shut the place down in October and fly south for the winter. He mock shivered. Can't take these winters anymore. That sounds nice. It is Don shoved his fingertips into his pockets. Well, I have to get over to the dining hall and make sure everything is running smoothly for breakfast. If you need help with all that trouble, you need help with all you just give me a shout, okay? She nodded. He turned on the hell of his batered running shoes and started back the way he'd come. Don? He paused and looked over his shoulder. Thanks. He smiled and offered her a thumbs up. Just doin my job, ma'am. And helping out a fellow passenger on the journey. She turned back toward the cabin. The nail polish on her toes needed replacing if she was going to wear open toed sandals all day. Doin his job? Had Carlos simply been doing his job, as well? All the talk of firefly wishes and kissing her, had that been just a psychologist working an emotionally fraught situation? She slamemed the screen door shut behind her. Then Nellie hesitated on the blue cabins porch step. The cool morning breeze stirred the chimes, creating a metallic clinking. Was having breakfast with Carlos a good idea after last night? Did she really want to put herself in that position? On the other hand, Carlos and Rose could act as a buffer against all those other people she had to face this morning, the ones who'd seen her make a fool of herself yesterday afternoon. Squaring her shoulders, she marched across the porch, drawing to a halt once again outside his door. I did not kiss her, not that it's any of your business. Carlos voice carried through the open front windows onto the porch. But Cherry said I don't care what Cherry said or what she thinks she saw last night, Last night? Nellie's cheeks tingled. Carlos groaded. Maybe we need to establish some ground rules.

I, as the father here will kiss whome ever I want, when ever I want. You, as the daughter, will not kiss anyone until you're a heck of a lot older, and then only father approved boys who are kind, afraid of me and germ free. Eeww, I don't want to kiss some icky boy. Thank God came Carlos soft mutter. Nellie covered her mouth with her hand and tried to swallow the laughter threatening to erupt. But I don't mind if you want to kiss Miss Nellie. I like her. A small burst of warmth blossomed in the center of Nellie's chest, but she wasn't sure if it was because Rose had given her father permission to kiss her or because the child liked her. Maybe a combination of the two? Another masculine groan reached her ears. I am not having this conversation with my eight year old. Nellie leaned closer toward the window I think its great, dad. Does this means you're takeing her on that date? We are not going on a date. A surprising wave of disappointment washed over her, dissipating the pleasant warmth. Not that she intended to date him but still, that stung. Obviously she'd been right. His wish for a kiss had been a fabrication, a psychologist handling a distraught woman in whatever way he thought would work. But what about the dinner you won? You can't waste a whole dinner. And Miss Nellie would be disappointed. She probably worked real hard to keep up with you so you would win. A bittersweet smile curved the left corner of her lips upward. Rose, champion of wounded women. The child was all spunk. Rose, hold still. Ow! Dad, take it easy, that hurts! It wouldn't if you'd hold still. Come over here. Ow! Stop. Through the window Nellie saw Carlos, his hands tangled in his daughters hair as he pulled her toward the kitchen counter. A memory from a long time ago surfaced. Nellie slammed the door into the far wall as she charged into the cabin. Don't do that. Let go of her hair! Carlos pauded, one arm outstretched in the direction of the counter, the other hand??? clutching strands of Rose's hair. I said let her go? If I let go I'll lose what little progress I've made on this french braid. Amusement sparkled in his brown eyes. How about handing me that comb? French braid? Nellie's knees went wobbly and she glanced down at Rose, whose eager face beamed a wide grin at her. You're braiding her hair? She passed him the black comb from the counter. Add ability to french braid a little girls hair to the list of amaaging things about this man. What did you think I was doing? Carlos deftly retrieved a strand of hair, then clenched the comb between his teeth and began weaving. When I saw you pulling on her hair, it reminded me... Nellie shook her head. I–I...never mind. You bust into my cabin and I don't even get an explanation? He muttered around the plastic. Nellie glanced back at the wide open door. I'm sorry. I'm just thought. Carlos plucked the comb from his mouth. You thought I was hurting her. Didn't you? She was yelling ouch. You came to rescue me from my mean, hair pulling father! With a giggle, Rose squirmed free from hher father's grasp and flung her arms around Nellie's waist. Carlos thew his hands into the air. Rose! Okay, that's it. Forget the french braid. Which, by the way, was your idea to start with, he reminded his daughter as he deftly undid the beginning of the complicated braid. Now you can have a ponytail what'll it be? The little girl backed away from Nellie and glanced up at her. Ponytail like Miss Nellie's. Nellie smiled at the child, the pleasant warmth creeping back into her chest to replace the burning embarrassment she'd felt only moments before. Difinitely easier than a french braid. I'll say, Carlos murmured. In a flash, his daughters hair was styled. There. He glanced over Rose's head. Have you decided to join us for breakfast? Nellie nodded. Good. Carlos watch beeped, followed immediately by a chiming from the one on Rose's wrist, Nellie arched an eyebrow and inclined her head at him. Medicine time, he explained, going to the kitchen cabinet. Rose has to take her meds on time for them to work the best, so, we do 7:30 am; and 7:30 pm. Meds? To keep my body from rejecting my new heart. All right, ladies, lets go. Carlos ushered them out side. They strolled leisurely along the dirt road, Rose skipping on a head. You were quite a sight, busting into my cabin like that. Nellie flushed and ducked her head. I'm sure I was. I can't seem to do much right these days. I think it was very it was very brave of you to intervene. Carlos stopped walking. But you should know that Rose is my life. I'd never do anything to hurt her. I do know that. But...But it looked bad, I'm sure. Who pulled your hair? He cast her a side ward glance and started walking again, small clouds of dust kicking up around his brown dock shoes in the wake of each step. She shook her head. Department of Defense dependents. My father was military man. Oh. That explains a lot. Up ahead? Rose squatted down on the side of the road? Obviously fascinated by something she'd discovered in the dirt. It does? Like what? Like how you keep everything bottled up inside you. I'll bet emotions weren't shown much in your house, were they? No. We all had to be good, soldiers. And how did your father feel about a teaacher who pulled his bids hair? Dad believes in discipline, but he also believes in fair play. Luckily I happened to be on the right side in that little misunderstanding. But dad reminded me that soldiers didn't cry, thaat I'd worried my mother with my crying. Bet that teacher didn't pull your hair again. Definitely not. Dad! Rose came running back down the dirt road in their direction, hands cupped together, arms extened out this time, Unsinkable? She skidded to a halt, tilted her head to the side and scowled at her father. Da-a-ad. Her sneakered foot stomped into the ground, creating a large cloud, and she jerked her head in Nellie's direction. Not in front of other people, remember? Sorry. Whatcha you got? Carlos leaned over for a better look. Rose sighed and extended her cupped hands and a toad jumped out, landed on the powdery road, then quickly hopped back into the underbrush. Oh, no! Carlos shook his head as he straightened up. We're on our way to eat. Toads and other critters carry germs, Rose sighed and extened her now empty hands toward her father. I know, but he was so cute, I just wanted you to see him. Not before we eat, okay? He reached into the pocket of his faded denim shirt and retrieved a small elastic bottle then squeezed hand sanitizer onto Rose's outstretched palms. Sorry, Rose mumbled, rubbing her hands together vigorously. Its all right. Just remember to go into the bathroom, and wash them when we get to the dining hall, okay? The recapped bottle disappeared back into his shirt pocket. He reached out and tucked a loose strand of her hair behind her ear. I'd say you qualify as one of the good surprise. You're not what I expected to find at summer camp. Dad! Rose yelled from the doorway of the main building. Hurry up! Cherry is already here! That's my daughter, always impatient. We old folks are far too slow for them. Daniel had two speeds supersonic and warp. That's rose these days. She held her hands up and grinned at her father. Ok, Dad? I'm gonna go say hi to Cherry. Carlos nodded his approval and began to follow his daughter. Nellie paused in the entry way. The scents of bacon and eggs made her mouth water, but she hesitated when several people glanced over at her. She backed up a step but stopped when a large, warm hand slipped over hers. Nellie. Carlos squeezed her fingers lightly. You promised me breakfast this morning you're not reneging on that, are you? I said maybe. Consider me a kid. I think maybe means yes. He pulled gently on her hand. Come on, you have to eat. His eyes once again conveyed his understanding of her reluctance and he offered his strength through his warm fingers now enterwined with hers. And you have to face them all at some point. Might as well be now. Spoken as a counselor? No spoken as a friend. Several slow seconds ticked by while she stared into his eyes. Then she squeezed his fingers back. Thank you. My pleasure. A spark glinted in the caramel depths. Shall we? He released her and gestured toward the breakfast line. She nodded and took one step into the room. The clapping began. First one woman at the closest table, then it spread to those near her. Then the woman rose to her feet. Nellie froze in place. Surely they weren't applauding her? The scene she'd made yesterday wasn't enough they were looking for an encore? More people rose to their feet. She could see their hands moving together, but a roar in her ears blocked out the sounds. Her chest tightened. Trudy's words from her office upon her arrival came back. They'll consider you a hero. Her throat closed and she struggled to breathe. A woman left one of the tables over by the windows and hurried to her, head and eyes lowered as she closed the gap between them. Nellie recognized her as the sharp tongued woman who'd asked for her credentials and started the whole messy spiral. Nellie? She didn't wait for a response. Honey, I just wanted to say how sorry I am about yesterday. I had no idea Nellie clinched her hand into a fist, trying to resist the overwhelming urge to pinch the bridge of her nose or better yet, to remove herself from the room as quickly as possible. Carlos gently pressed his hand into the small of her back. Gratitude for his support washed over her. Thank you. She focused on the woman as she said it, but the words were meant for him. The woman removed a green ribbon pin from her shirt. Her fingers trembled as she quickly placed it on Nellie. I want you to have this. It's for organ donation awareness. Nellie glanced down. The green stood out starkly against her white blouse. The pin weighed down her heart like a heavy stack of textbooks. Ok, no, I couldn't please I want you to wear it in honor of your little boy. She grabbed Nellie's hands for Daniel. Unable to speak, Nellie nodded and shook the womans hand, then whirled and buried her face in Carlos chest drawing comfort from his closeness. He wrapped his arms around her and held her tight. Easy, he whispered. Its ok. They're just trying to show you how much they appreciate what you did. Nellie trembled. She'd done nothing, she was no hero, no selfless person who'd tried to save other peoples lives when her son died. She was a complete fraud. She hadn't wanted to donate Daniel's organs in the first place. Rose's mouth watered. She darted another quick glance over her shoulder to check on her dad, then returned her attention to Cherry's breakfast. Give me a bite. She opened wide and leaned in closer. Her friend popped a square of the sweet, gooey stuff into her mouth. Mmm. Rose hummed, eyes closed. French toast was just short of heaven in her book. Too bad her father didn't find it nutritious enough. When she opened her eyes, she discovered Cherry's mom giving her a knowing look. Rose silently begged her not to tell. Thanks guess I'd better go and get my own food now. She headed off toward the buffet line, wishing for more than one bite of sweetness, but knowing she'd end up eating a gluey blob of heart healthy oatmeal. By the time she returned with her tray, her dad Miss Nellie were just sitting down. Nellie slowed as he whipped out a bleach towelette and scrubbed down the table in front of the space beside Cherry, Makeing sure she arrived at the table after he'd finished his embarrassing actions. How was he supposed to impress Miss Nellie when he acted like that? She was going to think he was a nutcase which in some ways, he was. Oh, good, Rose here, you sit next to Cherry. Rose slid into her place, nudging her friend in the process and rolling her eyes. Cherry tried to stifle a snicker, but ended up snorting like a pig. She quickly covered her mouth with a napkin and they both giggled. They sat in silence for what seemed like several long minutes. With her spoon, Rose picked the lumpy oatmeal that clung to the sides of the blue bowl.

Scooping up a small portion, she turned it upside down to check the thickness. The blob didn't move, even with a shake to encourage it. This stuff was far worse than the oatmeal her father made at home. You're not eating. Her dad said softly. She looked up, the words to defend her finicky behavior waiting on the tip of her tongue, and discovered, to her surprise, that his comment as well as his attention was diricted at Miss Nellie. Oh. The woman looked started as if she'd forgotten the food sitting before her. She glanced down at the plate. Oh, she said again, I didn't get a knife. She nudged the tray forward slightly. Or a napkin. A deep sigh escaped her. Dad jumped to his feet. Not to worry. I'll get them for you. He brushed his hand lightly over Miss Nellie's shoulder. You stay here and start on that bowl of fruit. You don't need a knife for that. Rose waited until he'd left before spearing the final peice of french toast off Cherry's plate and quickly eating it. Did you like the fireflies last night? Miss Nellie looked over at her. Yes, I did. Very much. I think that was the nicest present any one's given me in a long time. A tingly feeling spread from Rose's stomach across her chest. Miss Nellie's pretty hazal brown eyes held her's. Better than the marshmallow? The tiniest bit of a smile started in the corner of Miss Nellie's mouth. Definitely better than the marshmallow. Did you make some wishes? Miss Nellie nodded. Good you don't have to tell what they were. Thank you. Rose's dad returned and doled out the knife and napkins he'd gotten. Leaning over the table, he peered into her bowl. That oatmeal looks more like wallpaper paste. He held out a glass of milk. Here, Rose. If you stir some in, it should make it better. Tastes like paste, too. She made a funny face at him, then accepted the glass from him as he chuckled. I hope this helps. Eat, her dad commanded, first her, then he swung to include Miss Nellie. You, too, good health starts with good nutrition, and although I wouldn't call that he gestured at the french toast on her plate good nutrition, I'm willing to settle for you to eat anything. Is that what have to get something good, stop eating? Rose muttered, stirring the milk into the oatmeal. What was that? Dad asked. Nothing. Cherry's mom handed the baby to Eddie here, take him so I can eat down now. Eyes wide, Rose watched Miss Nellie down her french toast in the skicky syrup. Her own spoon reluctantly dug into the oatmeal. A woman in a white tank top came up behind Miss Nellie and laid a hand on her shoulder I'm sorry about your son. I just wanted you to know that, I admire your courage. The woman patted her then moved away quickly. Miss Nellie pushed the plat forward on the tray and sighed. Dad always said talking about bad things could make you feel better. How did your son die? Rose! The other adults at the table chorused. Her father glared at her, and Cherry pinched her thigh under the table. Rose kept her attention on Miss Nellie's. You apologize right now, young lady!

Carlos admonished. No, Nellie said no? She doesn't have to apologize. She asked the one question you all want the answer to. The weight of their stares made her stomach quiver, but it was Rose's eyes a hazal just a shade darker than her fathers that Nellie focused on. There was no pity in those sparkling eyes, only the natural curiosity of a child. She inhaled deeply and folded her hands on her lap. It was the first nice spring weekend. Daniel's dad took him to the playground. There was a big, wooden struture shape like a castle, and he loved going there. But he climbed somewhere he shouldn't have and he fell and hit his head. Did it hurt? Did he cry? I wasn't...there, but no, I don't think he cried. And don't think he felt anything. At least, that was the belief she clung to. She needed to believe there'd been no pain f or him. His brain was hurt too badly, I think. And that was why he died? His brain was hurt too bad? Nellie's throat tighten, and she wrung her hands beneath the table. Mist gathered, ofscuring her view of the somber freckled faced child across from her. She lowered her gaze and nodded. Warmth tingled the skin of her left thigh as Carlos fingers skimmed its surface, and then he latched on to her hand beneath the table and squeezed it hard. She squeezed back. The small island of silence at their table was surround by an ocean of happy chatter and occasional laughter only the baby stirred at their table, wriggling and cooing in his fathers arms. Wanna trade freak fasts with me? What?? Nellie's head popped back up and she looked across the table again, blinking to rid herself of the stubborn tears. Rose eyes twinkled at her. Trade. You eat my oatmeal, I get your french toast. She darted a quick glance at her father. Nellie pushed the tray toward her. Go ahead, you can have it. I'm not very hungry. Absolutely not! Carlos released her hand and retrieved her tray. Rose just pulling your leg. And you are both going to eat, and I mean now. Nellie opened her mouth to protest, but he pressed his finger against her lips. No excuses. Now eat. He dragged his fingertip. Across the fullness of her lower lip as he pulled his hand away. Igniting a slow smolder that had nothing to do with hunger. For food, anyway. Those concern filled eyes remained fixed on her mouth as he reached for her fork. Open, he ordered. Of its own accord, her mouth obeyed, and he slipped the fork past her lips. Sweet syrup and cinnamon. A sweet man and a spunky child. His intense gaze on her mouth. There was no moonlight to blame this time, but all she could think of was the last time his eyes had been on her like that, and his wish for a kiss. Michelle coughed loudly, drawing Nellie's attention back to the table. Cherry, you're finished, right? The older girl nodded. Okay, let's go. No Eddie give me the baby, then you can take our trays. Nellie snatched her fork from Carlos hand and bent over her food, cheeks heating at the direction of her thoughts. Obviously those thoughts had been clear enough that the other woman had been able to see them. We'll catch you later, jimbo, Eddie said, slapping Carlos on the shoulder as he rose to pick up the trays. You playing in the pool tournament this afternoon? I am. And you're going down. Eddie chuckled. We'll see about that. He headed off toward the garbage cans. Cherry followed him. Michelle gathered scatered baby supplies into a diaper bag with one hand. Dad, can I go too? Maybe Mrs Michelle will french braid my hair for me before activities start. Rose grinned at Nellie, then offered a saucy wink. Nellie forced her lips together, hard. A smile now, with a mouthful of french toast, would be a messy thing. All gone. Rose held her bowl up side down to demonstrate. Go. Her father waved. But stay with Cherry, and I'll check to make sure you're at your first activity on time.

Yeah! Rose bolted from the table, tray in hand, following after her friend. Cherry, wait! I'm coming with you. Good luck in gettin her to hold still for the braid, Michelle. I'd advise you just to say no and leave her with a ponytail. I know what I'm doing, Carlos. As Michelle leaned over to brush a kiss on his cheek, Nellie caught a whiff of baby powder. Her chest tightened with longing and she reached out to caress the babys chubby knee. Soft baby skin, like silk, met her touch, and David kicked his legs. I know what I'm doing, too, Michelle. Just checking. In seconds, Carlos and Nellie were alone at the table. Again. Well, Nellie said. Looks like I've done it again. Cleared the table. She watched Michelle sashay out the door. I don't think your friend likes me very much. It's not that she doesn't like you...Carlos began. Then what is it? He leaned closer and whispered, She's worried about me gettin involved with you. Oh, God. Forget food. Nellie swallowed the lump in her throat. And...are you? Am I what? His fingers found their way back to her face, he cupped her chin with on hand, and the index finger of the other brushed at the corner of her mouth. Get...getting involved with me? He moved his head away from hers. Well, involved is such a strong word, we're friends, right? She nodded. Although, their is thatmatter of my wish last night....He touched the edge of her lip. You're sticky again. It's not marshmallow this time. He inserted the tip of her finger into his mouth, closing his lips around it. Nellie was sure the heat scorching through her body was going to set the wooden bench on fire, and before they knew it the whole camp would go up in flames. That would look great in the report to Jerry, wouldn't it? He watched, captivated, as he removed his finger from his mouth. Nope. Not marshmallow. Syrup. He quickly glanced around the room, and lowered his voice further. And I want...What? He hesitated. To kiss her. God help me, I still want to kiss you. A whimper lodged in her throat. God help them both, because at the moment she'd like nothing more than to make his firefly wish come true. Unbelievable. She'd lived in the shadow of Daniel's death for so long that she'd forgotten what it felt like...to be alive. Maybe Camp Firefly wishes really was a place of miracles. Suddenly she caught sight of a flash of orange. She backed away from Carlos. His eyes widened in surprise as she groaned. What? Trudy and Don are staring at us. She smiled weakly at them. Trudy smiled in response, but Don folded his arms across his chest and squared his shoulders, reminding her very much of her father. I didn't believe it. Believe what? All these kids, all these people around us, and I let you make me forget all about them. Blast? So? Its not like we actually kissed or anything. I doubt they'll fire you or anything. Fire me, she whispered, then sighed heavily as the reality of her sutuation thundered back to her. At the moment, Don didn't look like a man inclined to give her a great report. They might not, but...But? Never mind. She rose from the table. Thanks for the breakfast company. Thats what friends are for, he called after her as she beat a hasty retreat. Good soldiers also knew when to fall back and form a new line of defense. Ongoing ping-pong games filled the sunny rec room, and around three other pool tables were several other parents who'd entered the tournament this afternoon. Although, the so called tournament had quickly disintegrated into individual games with no resemblance of organization. Carlos found it hard to focus on the game. Instead, his thoughts were zipping back and forth in time with the ping pong ball behind him. What the hell had he been thinking this morning in the dining hall? The urge to kiss Nellie, to lick the sticky smears from her pink lips had been overwhelming, and he just couldn't fingure it out. Okay, so she was pretty, and sweet, and damn it to hell if she didn't just twist his heart with her quiet, stubborn strength in the face of her loss....But almost kissing her with all those people looking on? If he didn't know any better, he'd claim to have lost his mind. But he did know better. People who thought they were crazy generally weren't. So how did he explain the whole thing? It was brave of you to let Rose signup for the bungee jumping. You know, Cherry really wanted to do that, but that was where Michelle drew the line. Instant panic, ice hot, speared his chest, then spread. Moisture slicked his palms. Bungee jumping? What the hell are you talking about? Carlos snapped his head up to glare at his friends grinning face. Bastard he mumbled low enough for their ears only. You are one sick bastard, you know that? Eddie roared with laughter. I had to get your attention somehow. You've got it bad, Jimbo. That obvious, huh? A blind person could see it, its that obvious. Carlos groaned.

Great. Raising his shoulder, he wiped a bead of sweat off the side of his face. Humid air hung heavy in the room as the old woodden ceiling fans worked hard to create a small breeze. Eddie leaned over the table, lining up his next shot. Eight ball, in side pocket. He pulled back the stick and let fly. The cue ball kissed the edge of the eight ball, sending it neatly into the pocket. It is great. He laid the stick on the table. I win. Third time in a row, you want to concede defeat, or shall I rackem up again? I'm not glutton for punishment. Carlos turned and replaced his cue into the rack on the wall. Which is why this is a bad idea. Playing pool? Playing period. Oh. Eddie nodded wisely. You know what they say about all work and no play, jimbo? Yeah, it makes Carlos a dull boy. Wrong. Eddie slipped alongside him, replaceing his own cue and the chalk cubes, and dropped his voice. It makes Carlos a love starved man. It's about time you found a woman to light your fire again. Great, between you and my parter cord, I've got a cheerleader in favor of this. Let's get out of here. It's stuffy. Maybetheres a breeze outside. Lead on. Carlos blinked against the bright sunshine as they headed out the door. Laughter came from the soccer field across the road as a group of kids played under the watchful eyes of several counselors. Carlos and Eddie strolled in the direction of the lake. Rose loves it here. She's haveing a lot of fun. I'm glad you guys could be here, too. She's missed Cherry. Cherry has missed her, too. But I gotta tell you, I'm just as happy not to see your face every weekend anymore. No offense to you, But I got tired of the hospital. I hear you. I love children and all the doctors and nurses, but I'd just as soon never set foot in there again. Which won't happen, with their biopsies and whatnot. Carlos sighed. That's the truth. And that's exactly why I can't get involved with a woman. Any woman. Involved? Who said any thing about getting involved? Eddie bent to retrieve a flat rock from the sand and skipped it out across the lake, six hops before it sank beneath the surface. Did't you ever have summer romances, jimbo? He grinned. Short term, no strings, and they leave you with the sweetest memories for the rest of your life memories? The torch planted firmly in the sand at the beach entrance caught his attention, its flickering flames spouting black smoke into the heavy air. Memories of finding Nellie had it been only yesterday? Lying on the floor of her cabin flooded him. She deserves more than that, Eddie arm cocked back, he paused then lowered his hand. Aah. Is that how it goes? Maybe you ought to let her decide what she wants. And even if she does? How do I manage it with Rose? Why don't you start with that dinner you won? Eddie chuckled. How I wish I could have seen the race. But I was busy. And Eddie waggled his eyebrows. And there's your first clue, you find time when the kid is busy doing something else. The dinner. Rose been nagging me about that. She says I can't disappoint Nellie. So don't. Take her out, have a few glasses of wine, enjoy yourself. You remember how to enjoy yourself, don't you? I wonder if she does? Hmm. Carlos wondered that himself. She'd been through so much. And what do I do with my daughter while I'm off enjoying myself? Eddie sent another rock skittering across the lake surface. She has a sleepover with Cherry,

Naturally. Blond hair glinted in the sun as he shook his head. Do I have to teach you everything jimbo? Hell, Cherry has a sleepover at a friends at least once a week if I have any say in it. He grinned. The idea had merit, and I certainly was temping. The image of a seminormal, grown up evening glammered before him, a candlelit dinner with a pretty lady, maybe hold her close and dance...Maybe more? Was he super dad? Or there still part of him that was just a man? It could be exactly what Nellie needed, a chance to get away from the camp and all the reminders of transplants and her lost son. But did he dare leave Rose alone for the night? It wasn't as if he were leaving her with her grand parents while he worked with patients, this would be leaving her behind for a purely selfish reason. No, not selfish. For her. For Nellie. I'll think about it. Who knew summer camp had such temptations for grown ups? He certainly hadn't expected to face a dilemma like this. Was it time to think a little bit about himself? Nellie lifted her ponytail off the back of her damp neck, wishing she had a few bobby pin to keep it up. Splashes and laughter drew her attention to the olaympic size swimming pool where lessons and a game of tag appeared to be in progress. Maybe she could dangle her feet in the water, cool off a bit. Entering the fenced off area, she reached down and shucked her sandals, gathering them by the toe loops. The damp concrete was blessedly cool beneath her bare feet, the sharp seent of chlorine hung in the air, and Nellie wrinkled her nose as she scanned the area for the best place to dip her feet without getting in the way. Off in the corner, tucked in a chair beneath a large umbrella, Rose cradled a hard cover book on her lap. She blew at a stray strand of hair trailing down her forehead, then glanced from her book to the pool and all the splashing kids from her group. Pure, undisguised longing filled herround, freckled face. Her shoughder pulling upward slightly, then slumped back down in an laudible sigh. Nellie diverted her steps toward the little girl, who was looking decidedly unspunky at the moment. Hey. Rose how come you're not swimming with the rest of the group? Forget your bathing suit? I did. Nellie dragged another chair over and dropped down into it, sandals clutched in her lap. No. This time the sigh was audible. I'm not allowed. Not allowed? How come? Germs, Rose mumbled. Germs? Nellie sat up straeght. I can smell the chlorine from here. What germs could survive that? The little girl lifted one shoulder and let it drop. Ask my dad. I'm not allowed in publicpools since he saw some story on the news about germs that can live in them, even with chlorine. She brushed at the strand of hair now glued to her forehead with beaded sweat Nellie's heart went out to her. What is it with your father and germs? Remember those pills I took this morning? Nellie nodded. Well, theymake it easy for me to get sick. My body doesn't fight my new heart, but it doesn't fight germs. Too good, either. All transplant kids have to be careful. She could see, but obessive? I see a bunch of transplant kids in that pool right now. Tell me about it. Rose shoved a bookmark into her book and thumped the heavy volume closed. I guess that means you can't even put your feet in there, huh? That's what I was going to do. Nope. The droopy expression on the normally sunny face tugged at Nellie. This child was supposed to sit here and watch everyone else have fun? That was just too cruel. When is swimming over? Next activity is at four o'clock. Nature hibie. Nellie glanced at her watch. It was 2:24, that meant Rose had to sit here in the heat for more than an hour before the rest of the kid's climbed from the pool. Tell you what, why don't you come with me instead of sitting around here? Where are you going? I was thinking about heading back to my cabin to pin my hair up off my neck, and then I'm going to find some other way of cooling off. Hopefully that bag of ballooms shed ysed for a science experiment was still buried at the bottom of her teaching bag. She didn't recall taking it out, but that didn't mean anything these days. Like what? Rose asked, he face brightening slightly Oh, I don't know. I guess you'll have to wait and see. What do you say? I say, what are we waiting for? Then lets tell your counselor that you're going with me and get out of here. Nellie slipped on her sandals. On the way out the gate, Rose reached for Nellie's hand. Nellie's heart skipped a beat then thudded against her chest as she wrapped her fingers around the childs smaller ones. She quickly chasedaway the dull ache, the empty void that grabbed her. Life moved forward, and so would she. She had to, or lose what she had left. Rose grinned up at her. Nellie smiled back and squeesed the little hand tucked inside hers. Carlos trudge up the dirt lane toward his cabin. Even the birds had gone silent to the heat of the afternoon, but as he got closer to the end of the lane, he heard muffled shouts and...laughter? A few high pitched giggles were punctuated by rough chuckles, rustty laughter followed, laughter that sounded more natural this time. Wait a minute. He recognized that voice and the giggles. They belonged to his daughter who was suppose to be with her group at the pool, not here. Carlos picked up this pace striding around the side of the blue cabin. Rose, what are you doing. Dad, look out! A flash of yellow hurtaled inchs in front of his face. Carlos stopped abruptly what's going on here? Rose stepped out from behind a bush. Straggly, drippy hair framed her face, and her pink t shirt clung to her chest. Her formerly white sneakers and socks were spattered with dirt in her hand, she held a round blue object. We're just having a water balloon fight. Wanna play? Rose smiled sheepishly and extended the balloon in his direction, We? He scanned for the other culprit, the source of the rusty laughter, and saw no one. He turned back to his daughter. You're wet? Why aren't you with your group? Carlos snatched the water balloon from her hand. Where did you fill these? Its my faucet. Don't be mad at her. Across the small glade, Nellie stepped from behind the corner of her yellow cabin, one hand held in front of her. One snaked behind her back. Do you realize that she's all wet now? That was the idea, yes. WE were just trying to cool off since she couldn't go in the pool. She can't go in the pool for a reason! Where did you fill these balloons? Nellie crossed the open area between them, stepping around spattered pieses of colorful latex. Calm down. We used the tap water. No big deal. Carlos whirled on his daughter. Rose, you get inside, get those wet clothes off and jump in the shower. Look at you. Your legs are filthy. Rose's lower lip trembled. I'm sorry Dad. She turned and ran toward the cabin. Carlos jammed his hand into his hair. Rose, honey, he called after her. Wait! She skidded to a halt, then slowly pivoted on the rubber tip of her sneaker. I'm careful because I love you. She balled her fists and propped them on her hips. Sometimes I think you love me too much! Her muddy foot pounded into the ground Maybe it's a good thing I don't have a mom, because with two parent's like you, I'd really smother! The screen door slammed as she raced inside. A slow ache built inside him. Smother? Was he really smothering her? No. He had her best interests in mind. Her health. But it hurt to hear her say he loved her too much. How could you love a person too much? He took a step in the direction of the cabin but stopped at the touch of a warm hand on his elbow. Let her go. Give her a chance to cool off. Carlos inhaled deeply, then exhaled forcefully. I don't understand the big deal. It was tap water. Nellie's soft voice drifted across his shoulder. Tap water can be contaminated, too. Not to mention when you mix it with mud...He whirled to face her...And forget Ros'es harsh words. Nellie's white blouse bore the evidence of his daughter's good aim, the moisture rendering it transplant in the bright sunshine. Lace cupped curves beckoned from beneath the material. He curled his fingers toward his palms, the urge to touch her so strong, pins and needles shot clear up to his elbows. She stepped closer and her aroma further addled his senses, the faint scent of lemon mingled with the healthy smells of sunsine, water and woman. Suddenly he was grateful for the weight of his denim shorts, which although hot, hid his erection a lot better than canvas or parachute shorts would. You just sent her inside to shower in that same tap water. How much sense does that make? She asked gently. He lifted his gaze from the swell of her breasts and locked on her eyes, trying to clear the hormoneinduced haze from his mind. What? Same water? Why did you bring Rose here, Carlos? So she could have a normal summer, have fun. We were having fun until you came on like a bulldozer. She reached up and tucked a loose strand of hair behind her ear. The gesture made her breasts jut forward and Carlos bit back a groan. If she moved like that again, even denim wasn't going to contain him. I haven't laughed like that since....He jerked his head up, caught the fading light in his brown hazel eyes. Something that had nothing to do with hormones or lust. He reached out to brush his finger across her cheek. Since Daniel died? She nodded. You should do it more often. His fingers glided over the damp, smooth skin of her face, traced the shape of her jawline. You're very pretty when you smile. And god knows you deserve some fun and laughter. What about you. Carlos? When's the last time you did something fun, something impusive? She caressed the back of his wrist, rekindling the pins and needles sparking up his arm. You mean before now? He snaked his hand around her waist and drew her against him. She gasped, dropping the water balloon from her hand. It plopped onto the ground next to them. She tilted her head back, and he dipped his head to take possession of her mouth. He meant to go slow, easy, but at the first bit of pressure, she parted her lips for him, and he accepted the invitation, deepening the kiss slipping into her mouth with the tip of his tongue. Butterscotch. She tasted of butterscotch. He profed deeper. Nellie moaned softly into his mouth. His tongue teased and explored, driving rational thought faraway. He slipped his hand lower on her spine. Fingers splayed across her bottom, he pulled her closer, against the hard ridge of his arousal. He wants me. The knowledge caused a surge of power to rush through her, a heavy feeling of desirability femininity, intoxicated by that and the overwhelming heat generated by his mouth on hers, and by his erection jammed against her belly, she whimpered her distress when he pulled away from her. Only their heavy breathing filled the super charged air hanging between them Damn he finally whispered, fingers finding her face again. I'd say I'm sorry, but I'm not. I guess firefly wishes really do come true. Maybe we should have Rose catch more tonight? He cupped her chin. But now that I've had a taste of your sweetness, I'm going to wish for more than a kiss, Nellie. His pupils widened. A lot more. Do you understand me? Oh, god. She understood, all right. Trouble. A Big trouble. Get pregnant get married get hurt trouble. And yet, the idea of losing herself in his arms definitely had appeal. He'd sent her halfway to heaven with one kiss. What would he do if she gave him a chance? She swallowed hard. I...I hear you. Don't look so horrified about it. You'll damage my fragile ego. He leaned in colser again, wrapping his arms around her in what could pass for a casual hug if not for the sensual awareness between them. Nothing will happen if you don't want it to. Did that guarantee include not getting pregnant? His warm breath against her ear sent tingles racing up and down her spine. I want to know every thing about you. Nellie. He released her and stepped back, tugging on the hem of his polo shirt, Two damp spots indicated where her breasts had crushed up against him. What do you say we claim that prize we won and have dinner together Friday night? Damp spots? Nellie glanced down and heat scorched her cheeks. No wonder he'd come on to her she looked like an absolute hussy, a renegade from some bar's wet T shirt contest. She folded her arms across her chest. Are you asking ce on a date? His face paled in respone to the question. He looked as if he'd swallowed one of the water balloons. A date? I––um––well…Nellie recalled his early morning, adamant words to his daughter, words to the effect that he wasn't going to date her. Serves him right. Let's see him squirm out of this. She smiled. I think that's what they generally call it when a man asks a woman out to dinner. Then I guess I am, he said. Friday night. Friday night. She nodded. Its a date. Amazing how a man's reasoning ability went to hell the second all the blood rushed south of the belt line. At least, that's what he'd kept telling himself. Far easier to believe it had been the wet shirt and what was beneath it that had gotten him into trouble rather than the ache he'd seen in her eyes when she'd spoken about not laughing since Daniel's death. He reached for the after shave bottle propped on the sink, wincing as the lotion bit into his skin. Mmm, that smells nice, dad. Carlos turned to find Rose leaning against the door frame, the mischievous twenkle back in her brown hazel eyes, her cold shoulder treatment of him after the balloon incident obviously over. What are you up to, unsinkable? You have your things ready to go to

Cherry's for the night? His gut tightened at the thought of leaving her for the whole night. Grinning widely, she shook her head. Not yet. She pranced in the doorway. This is gonna be so cool, dad. Thank you so much! In the space of a heartbeat, she'd flung herself at him, wrapping her arms around his middle, pressing her cheek against the bare flesh of his stomach. He gently stroked her unbound hair, a surge of warmth kicking him in the center of the chest. The love of this amazing child should have been enough for him. Then why did he keep feeling to drawn to Nellie? You're the best dad in the whole world. Yesterday he'd smothered her, and today he was the best dad in the world? Remember that the next time I tell you go do something you don't want to do. Rose giggled and tipped her head back to glance up at him. Okay, right now you're the best dad in the whole world. That sounds more like it. He released her, spun her in the direction of the door and playfully swatted her behind. Get your things together. We have to be out of here in about five minutes to get you down to Cherry's so I'm back in time to meet Nellie. Ooh, dad's going on a date. She giggled again as she vanished out the door. Its not a——" He stared at his freshly shaved face in the mirror and sighed. Okay, okay, it's a date. He reached for his toothbrush. Hey! Come back here. You forgot your toothbrush, you little monkey! When Rose returned, he dropped to one knee. She reached for the toothbrush, but he held tightly to it. Are you sure you're okay with this, unsinkable? She rolled her eyes. Going to Cherry's? Of course No I mean, with me going on a date. Oh, daddy. She looped her arms around his neck and dropped her forehead against his. The soft scent of her hair rose around him. No longer the sweet smell of baby shampoo, but a floral fragrance. I want you to be happy. You take care of people at work and me at home. You deserve a bunch of date's if that's what you want. She pressed a kiss to the tip of his nose. Eyes closed he wrapped his arms around her and held her tight, she steady thump of her heart against his chest a reminder of the treasure the miracle she was. I love you. Rose. I love you, too, daddy. She wriggled in his arms and pushed away. Now, get a shirt on or you're gonna be late. She snatched the toothbrush from his hand and dashed from the bathroom once more. A few minutes later he checked his watch again, then pulled a cotton polo shirt from a hunger and yanked it over his head. Rose? You ready? She's ready, are you? Eddie asked from the bedroom door. What are you doing here? Carl tucked the bottom of the shirt into his jeans. I'm here to pick up Rose and make sure you get off okay. Eddie glanced over his shoulder. And I've brought you something. He entered the room and held out his hand. Take this. Carlos glanced down at the pager cradled in Eddie's palm. I don't need that, I've got my cell. But thanks. Trust me, you need this. Take it. Eddie pressed it into Carl hand. The weight didn't feel right. Carlos held it in his palm, then turned a quizzical glance to Eddie, who grinned, and popped open the mock pager. Revealing several condoms. Carlos shook his head. Getting a little a head of ourselves, aren't we? Hellno, this is your night, jimbo." I don't think so. His hormones protested, but he didn't want to expect that the night would land him in Nellie's bed. He still hadn't decided if that would be a small move or not. Besides, there was no guarantee and grinned at him as he pulled the plastic containers from the kitchen cabinet. I have my toothbrush and my pj's and my clothes for tomorrow. I'll remember to take a shower and put on clean underwear. I won't eat any junk food, and we'll go to bed at a reasonable hour. Did I forget anything? Seventhirty, he told Eddie, shoving the small plastic bag into his hands. Direction are on the labels, and Rose knows the drill, too. We're familiar with the routine, jimbo. Carlos turned to Rose. Sounds like you've got it all conered. I think you only forgot one thing. What's that? My good night hug and kiss. I guess I'll have to have them now. She dropped her backpack to the ground and entered his wide stretched arms. He stroked her hair for a moment, then bent over so she could place a loud kiss on his cheek. Night daddy. Night tiger. You be good. You have fun. She smiled at him. And make sure Miss Nellie has fun, too. I'll do my best. He turned toward Eddie. You have my cell number, and the number of the restaurant. We'll be fine, jimbo. Do make sure you both have fun. Eddie gave him a final wink before he ushered the girls out the door. See you at breakfast. The screen door slammed shut. Silence. The emptiness of the cabin washed over him, and he inhaled deeply. He had a whole evening ahead, an evening when he was to forget about being a dad and concentrate on beiong a man. He pulled his cell phone from its holder on his belt and opened it. Yeah, it's working. A light tap sound at the door. Carlos? Nellie. He glanced at his watch and hustled onto the screemed porch. Sorry, we got a little behind with getting Rose" He stopped mid sentence and stared. You look great. The turquoise of her sleeveless blouse set off her light brown sunshine hair and bright hazel brown eyes, and the tight denim capris she wore set off everything else. Including his hormones. A pretty flush rose in her cheeks. Thank you. She gave him a quick onces over before dropping her gaze. So do you. Okay, now they had the awkward complimenting stage over with. So far so good. He fished for that SUV key in his pocket. Our reservation are for seven. She dangled a set of keys from her index finger. I thought we'd take the goat. And I thought you might like to drive. He slapped his hand over his chest and groaned. Be still, my heart. You're not teasing, are you? It's not nice to tease a man, you know. I'm not teasing. She tossed the deys at him. A beautiful woman and a muscle car. He threw his head back and grunted. Testosterone overload, here I come? God, it felt good to be just a man. Nellie blinked a few times as her eyes adjusted to the dimly lit restaurant. Red and white checked table cloths covered the tables; flickering candles spilled melting wax down their wine bottle holders. Soft instrumintal music swelled in the back ground, and Nellie tried to swallow the dry sand in her mouth. Butterflies or maybe Rose's fireflies flitted in her stomach as Carlos took her elbow. What would they talk about now that the car topic had been exhausted? Small talk had never been her strong way. Right this way. With a smile, the young hostess clutched the menus to her chest and headed toward the back of the restaurant, weaving through the mostly unoccupied tables. The kitchen door opening as they passed, and the scent of freshly baked garlic bread wafted out. Nellie's stomach did a somersault. She stumbled. Carlos steadied her, You okay? Fine. She shrugged off his hand, squeezed her lips together tightly, and followed the hostess. After they were seated at a secluded table in a little back alcove and had placed their drink orders, Nellie studied the menu intently. What looks good to you? You do. But she didn't dare voice that opinion, even though it might have distracted her from the memories the little Italian place was threatening to bring to the surface. I don't know. What are you going to have? I'm not sure. Maybe the lasagna. No! The plastic menu holder clattered against the table top and Nellie folded her hands in her lap. You have something against lasagna? Sweat beaded on the back of her neck. Sorry. No you go ahead and order what you want. She could handle it. Forpitys sake, get a grip. It's just food. He set down his menu held out his hand expectantly. Tentatively, she unwound the linen napkins and placed her hand in his palm. Warmth infushed her as he closed his strong fingers around hers. Nellie, friends share. They don't bottle things up. He winked at her. Remember what I told you happens when you bottle things up? Yes you end up looking crazy and incompetent and on the brink of losing the only thing you have left. Only he'd put it more professionally something about ending up woth a stress related illness. So tell me, why don't you want me eating lasagna? The dim lightin soothing, sofa music and warmth from his hand made her feel safe. What do you call it when a person won't eat something because it made her sick once? A conditioned taste aversion? I have one of those to lasagna. He studied her intently, and she squirmed in her seat. It has something to do with Daniel, doesn't it? She bobbed her head slightly. It was his favorite. I was making it for him she cleared her throat. I had a batch in the oven, cooking, when Peter called to tell me Daniel had been hurt. Oh, god. Carlos squeezed her hand. I'm sorry, Nellie. Okay, no lasagna. He glanced around the restaurant. Are you sure you want to stay? Because we can go someplace else. We don't have to have dinner here. And lose our prize? She shook her head. No we worked hard for this dinner, and Rose cheered us on. Just so long as we stay away from the lasagna...You know, you can recondition yourself. You just have to pair the noxious stimulus with something pleasant. He lifted her hand and placed a light kiss in the middle of her palm. Something pleasurable. His mouth caressed her skin again. Heat rushed from the spot where the tip of his tongue teased gently to flood her entire body. If anyone could recondition her, it would be this man, this compassionate, tender, sexy man. Really? How does that work? His lips pressed against her wrist and she prayed he couldn't feel her heart racing. Well, you could take it in small steps. If, for example, you found you could tolerate being in an Italian restaurant and smelling lasagna, then you could move on. His chair grated against the floor as he moved closer. Then maybe you could try having some one eat it in front of you. Eventually you'd be able to eat it yourself. What–what about the other stimulure? You know, the pleasurable one? What would you choose for that one? That depends, he murmured, reaching to tuck a stray piece of hair behind her ear, then brushing the backs of his fingers over her cheek. On what? She whispered. On whether or not we were alone. She swallowed hard. And if we were? Holy mother of pearl, she was playing with fire. He leaned over, his words hot on her ear. Pleasure is so personal, Nellie. What's the most pleasurable thing you can imagine me doing to you? Her breathing went shallow, and her eyes closed as thoughts of his larger, gentle hands and mouth, oh yes, his mouth—all over her body sent a thrum of desire rushing through her bloodstream. Mmm, yeah, he whispered. What ever that idea is, I'd love to oblige, And she'd love to let him...If only she—Are you ready to order now? The waitress set their drinks on the table in front of them. Nellie jerked away from him, face scorching. Hopefully the dim light wasn't enough for either Carlos or the waitress to notice. Carlos smiled at her and squeezed her hand. She'd totally forgotten he was still holding it. I'll...I'll have the lasagna. His smile faded. You don't have to do that, Nellie. I mean, what I was saying is correct, but it takes time. It's not just a one shot attempt. I want you to enjoy yourself tonight. Lasagna was always a favorite of mine, too. I want to do this. Carlos shook his head. Damn, if half his patients had the courage of this women, his job would be a lot easier. Are you sure? She nodded. He turned toward the waitress. The same for me. They completed their dinner orders, and he sighed with relief when the waitress left them alone again in the dark corner. The flickering candlel light revealed apprehension in Nellie's hazal brown eyes. You can still change your order. I can, call her back. No. This is something I have to do. You are a remarkable woman, Nellie. And brave. (What he didn't know is that she wasn't brave, only her faith in god made her brave and all things possible for her) Her lips pursed together, and she shook her head. Hardly.

Totally. Coming to Camp Firefly wishes was an act of courage. Yeah, right. She removed her hand from his and lifted her water glass, taking a sip. It was an act of desperation, not courage. I don't understand. Explain it to me. He wanted to know everything about her, from her childhood in a military family, to what she was like as a teacher, to the exact image that had flashed through her mind when she'd closed her eyes and started breathing faster as he'd whispered in her ear. Especially that image. She broke off a piece of Italian bread and buttered it. I was kind of...Coached into coming to camp. In all honesty, it wasn't something I wanted to do. Because you weren't ready? He spread butter on his own slice of bread, watching her from the corner of his eye. Exactly. She offered him a slight smile. Its nice that someone finally understand. I understand, but I think you're under estimating yourself. Maybe you were ready but were afraid to admit it to yourself. Just as he didn't want to admit to himself how drawn he was to this woman, and not just on a physical level. Why would I be afraid? Maybe you feel that starting to deal with Daniel's death means losing him all over again. Is that your professional opinion, Doctor Carlos? Actually, yes. He leaned back in his chair waving his slice of bread in the air. But I have to remind you, we're not on a consultation here. We're—he swiveled his head, checking for listeners, and dropped his voice to an exaggerated whisper on a date. Her smile widened. Yes, we are. I'd nearly forgotten. Of course, it's been so long since I've been on a date, you'll have to excuss my rusty skills. I hear you. He chuckled softly. Care to compare? I'll bet mine are rustier. Really? Mouth full of bread, he nodded. I thought a guy like you would have plenty of dates. A guy like me? What's that supposed to mean? Running a finger along the woven edge of the basket, she looked down, and her cheeks final flushed. I don't know. You're kind off... The final word of the sentence was mumbleed under her breath. He propped his elbows on the edge of the table. What was that? Smooth. A ladie's man. He straightened up in the chair, puffing out his chest. Damn, there was a hell of a lot to be said for a testosterone rush. Who needed drugs or alcohol when hormones could do such a job? I know you don't mean that as a compliment, but that's how I'm taking it. He chucked. My partner would be on the floor, howling. The truth is my last date was about four years ago. And the only reason I remember is because Rose was four years old. Four years? Okay I win. My last date was six and a half years ago. Too bad my husband didn't stop dating at the same time. She propped her chin in her palm, eyes taking on a far away look. He cheated, huh? A flicker of hunt flashed in the brow depths as she nodded. I shouldn't have been surprised, given the reason for our marriage. And talk about a ladie's man? That was Peter to a T. I guess I always hoped he'd change. You know, he missed out on having a dad in his house growing up, and I believed him when he said he wanted to try to make our marriage work. Although, I think maybe Peter's real motivation was the possibility of my father or Jerry tearing his head off. The waitress returned with their salads, and Nellie fell quiet until the woman left again. Carlos stirred red vinegar into the mixed greens. Who's Jerry? Jerry's my principal. And Peter's uncle. He was not happy when he found out there was a baby on the way before a wedding. So he offered to marry you? Eventually. With a little encouragement. But we were the ones who made the final decision. Over their salads, Nellie explained how Peter had been summoned for a meeting in her fathers den a den she described as the ultimate male retreat, complete with gun cabinet and mounted hunting trophies. When he arrived, Nellie had been seated on the couch, and both her father and Jerry were present. After a brief interrogation, as Nellie termed it, the two older men handed the younger one a package containin two plane tickets to Las Vegas along with hotel and wedding chapel arrangements, all prepaid, And that's how I ended up a married woman. Peter and I discussed it, and decided it really was the best thing for all of us, for the baby, for me and my career. I guess it just didn't work out for him the way we expected. Did you love him? A burning densation developed in the pit of his stomach while he waited for the answer. Too many peppers in the salad. He pushed his not.-quiet-empty boul away. A pensive expression filled her face. I believed I was in love with him. Like many women, I thought my love could change him, heal him. She sighed. But I don't think I really understood what love was all about. Love is about sacrifice, and sticking around, and working things out. Love is being there through the hard stuff. My pregnancy was the first hard thing we faced, and I thought that since we passed that test we'd be okay. She smiled softly. That's enough about me. Tell me something about yourself. Well, you're right about love being about standing together through the hard stuff. Tiffany, my ex-wife, didn't get that either. Our marriage had been smooth sailing until we found out about Rose's heart defect in the second trimester of the pregnancy. His abs tightened, and he tried hard to brush aside the anger that still lingered. Nellie's fork fell to the table, and she reached for his hand. Then what happened? Tiffany's first instinct was to ask the doctor if it was too late for an abortion. He squeezed her fingers. Nellie's mouth gasped open for a moment, then she snapped it shut. I...I don't know what to say. Neither did I. Obviously you managed to convince her otherwise. Yes, thank god. He couldn't imagine life without the child who'd stolen his heart from the moment he'd first found out about her existence. Even at the ultrasound that had revealed the defect, he'd seen her a baby sucking her thumb as his child, counting on him to make everything right for her. But Tiffany didn't understand unconditional love. All she understood was that our baby ended up getting far more attention than she did, and that it was hard work to spend your days at a hospital bedside. So she left you and Rose? Carlos nodded. Her loss. The vehemence in the normally soft voice surprised him. Rose is a wonderful child and I can't imagine how a mother could turn her back on any child, let alone one with such a sunny personality. Does she have visitation rights? Only on paper. She lives in California now and doesn't have time for her daughter. Rose's lucky to get a card on her birthday and Christmas. That's awful. Genuine concern filled her expression. Your daughter is a special kid, Carlos. She's blessed to have you for a dad. And your ex obviously, got out of line when they were handing out maternal instincts. God, I'd give anything...Candle light glinted off the tears welling up in her eyes. She withdrew her hand, tossed her napkin on to the table and gathered up her purse. I have to go to the ladies room if you'll excuse me...He rose to his feet with her and laid a restraining hand on her arm. Don't be gone too long. I'll be lonely without you. Eyes down cast, she nodded. And I will come in there after you, if necessary. She glanced up at him through her long lashes, mouth still clenched in a tight line, and nodded again. Shrugging off his hand, she strode quickly across the restaurant. Several other diners, particularly the men, looked up as she passed their tables. A quick stab of jealousy pierced him. I'll be lonely without you? He sank back down into his chair. And jealously? What the hell was that all about? Caught you, Nellie said as she slipped back into her chair. Carlos returned the cell phone to its holder on his belt loop before he looked over at her. Her eyes were slightly puffy and tinged with red, but otherwise she looked fine. Caught me what? You were checking up on Rose, weren't you? Guilty. Nellie smiled and shook her head. Don't you trust your friends to take care of her? How is she? She? She's fine. Annoyed that I called, but fine. He studied her intently for another minute. What about you? Me? I'm fine. Why wouldn't I be? Do I need to give you a list? Do I need to remind you again about keeping things bottled inside? While she'd been gone, he'd asked the waitress to postpone bringing their food, until he was certain she was going to be able to handle it, knowing how important maintaining her composure was to her, he didn't think falling apart in Giordano's Italian restaurant would be good for her. He wasn't going to be much good for her, either, if he couldn't keep his mind off how much he wanted to sweep her into his arms, kiss her into a stupor, and then make love to her. You're nothing if not persisteent, Doctor Carlos. She fussed with the napkin on her lap. Don't call me that. I know how you feel about my profession, and besides, I told you, I'm off dirty tonight. Tonight I'm just Carlos, out on a date with a pretty lady who I already consider a friend. And I wish she'd feel the same about me. No. You're too special to be just anything. An intoxicating rush stormed him that had nothing to do with the glass of merlot he'd been sipping. Special. She thought he was special. He was treading deeper water than he'd expected. Hormones and lust were a helluva lot safer. Because he thought she was pretty special, too. He cleared his throat. Thanks. A ringing cell phone saved him from anything further on that topic line. A brief flash of panic dissipated as he realized it wasn't his. Nellie pulled a small phone from her purse. Hello? Her brows knit together. Hello? When no one answered her, Nellie looked at the caller ID. Blocked number. She stabbed the off button. A quiver ran along her spine. Who was it? Carlos asked. She shrugged. Nobody, I guess. She stuffed the phone back into her pocket book, unable to shake the feeling that it had been Peter. She glanced around the restaurant. Where's our waitress? I'm starving. Okay, if you're sure. Carlos signaled the waitress. Now, why don't you tell me what brought you to Camp Firefly Wishes? The waitress arrived setting plates of steaming lasagna in front of them and replacing their emty glasses with full ones. The scent of sauce mingled with garlic from the bread wafted to Nellie's nose and she forced down the over whelming sense of dread that accompanied the smell. She straightened her spine and firmly grasped her fork, poising it over the plate. Okay, I can do this. She glanced across the table. Did she dare ask him? The delightful teasing they'd engaged in earlier certainly would help make the food go down a lot easier. Besides, teasing and flirting didn't mean she was about to jump into bed with him. *Where's that other stimulus you promised? The pleasurable one?* One side of his mouth curved slowly upward. *We're not alone, but I'll see what I can do.* He took her left hand and turned it palm up on the red and white checked table cloth. His fingertips traced swirling patterns over the sensitive skin, wandering up over her wrist, back to her palm, to the ends of her fingers. Nellie closed her eyes and sighed. It had been so long since she'd been touched in anyway, not counting hugs from children. She craved adult human contact. His contact especially, she realized with a jolt. The scent of lasagna grew stronger and she opened her eyes to see Carlos holding a loaded fork. *You ready for this?* She opened her mouth, and he eased the food in. Her heart thudded against her chest, and her throat threatened to close off, preventing her from swallowing. She shut her eyes again and prayed not to embarrass herself. The fork clattered on to the plate and Carlos moved closer, his fingertips leaving her hand and slipping onto her thigh beneath the edge of the tablecloth. Warmth caressed her ear as he spoke softly. *I still don't know what that pleasurable image was you pictured earlier, but I'm game for later if you are.* The image returned, only this time with far more detail: skin to contact between their naked bodies; Carlos sensual mouth lingering ever her lips, her breasts, her...A wicked, wonderful sensation crawled over her. In an effort to clear the lump in her throat, she swallowed the lasagna without tasting it. She opened her eyes to find him watching her intently. You're game for later? Isn't that kind of risky with out knowing what I pictured? What if my image involved tying you up and having my wicked way with you? Heat flared in his eyes, and he grinned at her. He tightened his fingers around her leg. A man can always hope. His eyebrows moved up and down and a rich chuckle rumbled in his throat. But you don't stride me as dominating type. No? He shook his head. And I'm usually pretty perceptive about those kinds of things. Personality assessment goes with my job. So how do I strike you? She accepted another mouth ful of food from him. You strike me as a very sensual, sexy lady, someone whose idea of pleasure would be my pleasure to indulge. Sexy? He thought she was sexy? Even Peter's seduction had been more or less the result of a self challenge to see if he could corrupt miss goody two shoes. And he'd made it plain a few months into their marriage that he'd found her boring in the bedroom, that even his expert tutelage couldn't make her into something she wasn't. One of her acts of defence after the divorce was to buy herself a whole new set of lingerie. I see doubt in those beautiful hazel brown eyes, Carlos said, offering her more food. I mean it. You became one of my fantasies the moment we met. Fantasy? She managed to choke out. Really? He pressed his lips together tightly, as though suppressing a grin, and nodded. With Rose and work, I have neither the time nor inclination these days for much more than fantasy. And, lady, let me tell you, if the reality is half as good...His eyes darkened, and his cheeks flushed. She felt pretty flushed herself. No one had ever fantasized about her before. The reflection of the condlelight in his eyes illuminated a smoldering that had nothing to do with the flickering flame. Oh, yeah. Her initial assessment of him had been right. Trouble. And for once, inviting trouble didn't seem such a bad idea. He couldn't wait for the meal to end. Distracting Nellie from the painful memories triggered by the lasagna was driving him to distraction. She still their trembling, Carlos tightened his fingers around her thigh, resisting the temptation to stray a little higher. She inhaled sharply and froze in place, save for her widening eyes. Her pupils dilated, all but obscuring the brown of her irises. He swallowed hard and completely, stilled himself. Carlos. Nellie's voice held a breathy note of desire. Her body shifted slightly forward, pressing against his hand. He unglued his tongue from the roof of his mouth. Dam, Nellie. His heart pounded. He removed his hand from her leg and gripped the edge of the table till his knuckles turned white. She sighed, disappointment filling her eyes. He swallowed a groan. Nellie, if I don't get my hands off you, I'm never going to be able to walk out of this restaurant. You still might have to walk in front of me. Really? He nodded. Oh. Wonder and amazement rang in her whisper, leaving Carlos to ponder what kind of idiot her ex–husband had been to make her so question her potent sensuality. You sure made short work of this lasagna. The waitress scooped up the empty plates. Now, what can I get you folks for dessert? The tiny shake of Nellie's head told Carlos all he needed to know. He wanted to shout with joy. Nothing, thanks, just the check. That's all been taken care of. You folks enjoy the rest of evening and the rest of your time at camp firefly wishes. The young server tossed Carlos a saucy wink, then walked away. I'm sure we will. He dropped a few bills on the table. Shall we go? Oh, my god. Oh, my god! Henry! A woman's frantic voice carried from the from the front of the restaurant. Help! Oh, please, someone help him! Carlos chair rocked back and forth on its legs as he jumped up and dashed into the main dining room. A gray haired woman wrung her hands, standing over a still form on the floor. Carlos dropped to his knees beside the man. What happened? He asked, fingers already searching the man's neck for a pulse. I...I don't know. One minute he was fine, the next minute, he winced, rubbed his arm and fell over. Oh, help him, please! Somebody call 911" Carlos yelled at the other diners and staff who had already gathered. Tell them we've got a cardiac arrest. Recertified in cpr every year like clockwork, his training kicked in automatically. One paramedic issued a commands to other members of the first aid squad. Carlos circumvented the group to get to Nellie and the man's wife, who was now openly sobbing. Nellie patted the woman on the shoulder as they both watched the rescue efforts. Nellie...Both women looked up at him. Nellie's eye's flooded with relief. Carlos. This is Rosemary. "Oh, thank you, thank you for helping my poor Henry. The woman grabbed his hands and squeezed them. Clear! A paramedic yelled. The command echoed through Carlos head, and he shut out the images of the cardiac unit at children's hospital. Rosemary turned her head toward her husband just as they used the defifrillator on him. She flinched as Henry's body twitched. Oh! What are they doing to him? They're doing their best to get his heart going again. Carlos draped his arm around her shoulders and gently turned her around. Why don't we get you a seat over here, out of the way of the traffic? But I want to stay with Henry! You can help the rescue workers the most by staying over here. Carlos assisted the woman to a seat, and a squad member quickly appeared to ask questions about Henry. I've got a pulse! A paramedic proclaimed. A cheer went up around the restaurant, and Rosemary turned teary eyes at Carlos. She offered him a wavering smile and nodded her head in response to another question from the paramedic. As the adrenaline rush faded, Carlos knees turned rubbery, much like the woman's smile. He stumbled to a nearby empty table and sank down into a chair, propping his elbow's and covering his face with his hands. He breathed deeply, filling his lungs to capacity; he held the air in for a moment, then exhaled slowly. It could have been Rose. He wrestled the thought into submission by reminding himself that despite the fact he had taken the cpr training in case, god forbid, his daughter had needed it, he'd never actually used it before tonight. Rose was fine, and in the capable and also cpr trained hands of his friends. Her new heart was healthy and strong. Everything was fine. A warm hand closed around his left shoulder she's fine. I know. But thanks. He grabbed Nellie's fingers. How did you know what I was thinking? She leaned forward. I figured there was a reason you knew cpr so well, and I figured you'd be thinking about her, that's all. No psychic powers needed. Carlos rose from the chair, still clutching her hand. Good. You're amazing enough without adding special powers to the mix. Heled her back to Rosemary's side. The woman twisted the strap of her purse around her fingers as they loaded her husband onto the gurney. Do you think he'll be allright? She asked him. The heart is an amazing thing, Rosemary. It's a lot to ugher than most of us realize. Thank god for that. I'm sorry, ma'am but we've got two Emt's on board. There's not enough room for you. What? She twisted the bag's handle tighter around her hand. But...but how am I supposed to get to the hospotal? I can't drive now! Rosemary, it's okay. Carlos gently removed the woman's purse from her fingers. He nodded to the paramedic, who slammed the door of the ambulance. Sirens wailing, it charged out of the parking lot. Carlos turned back to the trembling woman where's your car? I'll drive you to the hospital and stay with you until your family arrives, okay? Tears filled the woman's eye's. Bless you! What a darling man you are. The keys are in my bag. Good. Carlos turned to Nellie. You follow us, okay? To...to the H–hospital? That is where they're taking Henry. Carlos accepted the keys from Rosemary. I'll see you there. O–okay, sure. He knew what it was like to be alone in a hospital while you waited for new's from a cardiologist about someone you loved. And he didn't want this woman to go through it that way. It wasn't until he was driving the old Buick down the road that he realized Nellie hadn't looked very enthusiastic about the idea. But Rosemary's sobbing didn't leave him time to think about it. Nellie's heart felt heavy in her chest as she pulled into the parking lot of the county hospital. Carlos, already out of Rosemary's car and standing in the circle of illumination from a streetlight, waved and pointed to the building, then escorted the older woman into the emergency entrance. Nellie cruised the lot, evaluating and discarding various empty spaces too close, too far, sandwiched between battered cars, too narrow. If she was lucky, she could play find–a–parking space until Carlos got Rosemary settled. But after ten minutes she tired of the game and slipped the convertible into a slot faceing the building. Her clammy fingers beat an erratic rhythm on the steering wheel, tempo increasing, then abruptly stopping. She jumped from the car and slammed the door. Her hands curled into tight fists, fingernails degging into her palms. You can do this. You ate lasagna tonight. You can do this. Lace those boots tighter and carry on, soldier. Stiff legged, she marched through three rows of cars, over the curb and onto the grass, then finally the side walk. She paused beneath a droopy maple tree to study the squat, four story building across the road. He'd called her amazing and brave. The nurse at the reception desk scribbled information from a man cradling his towel wrapped hand in his lap. Nellie swallowed hard and moved toward the waiting area. Blue plastic chairs hard looking, not meant to be inviting, Small tables cluttered with magazines sporting tattered cover and pamphlets about various disease. In the corner of the room, a television blared cnn more crime, more disease, more bad news. One phrase Nellie caught as she pressed against the wall. Severe head trauma was another. Severe. Head trauma. A loud roar filled her ears. In her mind, she could hear those same words from a different doctor. And later he'd said brain dead. Her legs trembled as other voices invaded, a stranger, a soft spoken woman. We'd like to talk to you about organ donation Peter: I think we should, Nellie. Her father: It makes sense, Nell. She hadn't wanted it. Couldn't face the thought of them cutting into her baby. She wanted to gather him into her arms despite all the tubes and wires and kiss the boo–boos away. They'd left her alone with him for a while. She smuggled down next to him on the hard, uncomfortable bed; fixed his ash brown hair so the bandage on the side of his head wasn't as noticeable, ran her fingertips over his cheeks. He looked so peaceful, her baby, an angel in waiting just like the country music song said. She knew she needed to say goodbye and give him permission to fly. It had been so hard to get past the fact that if you didn't count the tubes and such, he looked as if he'd wake up from his nap any minute, throw his arms around her neck and kiss her. Then ask her if she wanted to play cards with him. Her father leaned over the bed and informed her it was time to go. Daniel, four and a half years old. Goal in life, to go to kindergarten on the big yellow school bus like the kids his mom tought. He hadn't made it. Tears leaked from the corners of her eyes, tears she hadn't dared she'd that day in her father's presence. They slid down her face, collectin under her chin, in her throat. Her heart hammered against her breastbone. Her breath came in quick gasps overloading her with the smells of the hospital despite a rapidly clogging nose: the cleaners, the disinfectants. Death. Blackness ofscured the edges of her sight, creating a tunnel vision effect. Far off in the distance, Carlos turned and looked at her, then he, too, faded into darkness.

Nellie! Carlos nearly knocked Don over as he dashed down the corridor. Nellie! He repeated, then watched as she slid the rest of the way down the wall and crumpled into a heap at its base. He dropped to his knees on the hard floor and gathered her into his arm, reassured by the pulse beneath his fingers on her teardampened throat. Nellie? Come on, get back here. How much you want to bet this is her first time in a hospital since she lost her son? Don asked, bending over them both. Dammit, I never even thought about that. Carlos slapped her cheeks. Come on, Nellie I need smelling salts here! I didn't picture her as a fainter. I thought she was dealing with all of it better than this. Carlos glared up at him. She's doing great. Tonight she over came a conditioned aversion relating to her son's death. Jeez, give her a break. Weren't you the one who told me to stand back and hope she popped? Well, she popped, all right? Nellie? Come on sweetheart, wake up. A nurse in pink scrubs knelt next to him and waved an ammonia capsule under Nellie's nose. She inhaled sharply and turned her head away. The persistent nurse followed her with the smelling salt. Nellie moaned, her eyes fluttering open. Then she began to cough. No. Get it away. Bring that wheel chair over here. An orderly promptly obeyed the nurse, wheeling the chair beside Nellie. No. Let me out of here. Gotta get out. Nellie shoved at the nurses hand. Easy, Nellie, everything's allright. Relax and let us get you in this chair. You can lie down for a few minutes and you'll feel much better. She struggled to sit up. No. You don't understand. I can't stay here. Not a minute longer. Nellie struggled to her feet and made for the doorway. The nurse shook her head and walked off, no doubt to find a patient who better appreciated her. Don made a sympathetic clucking sound. He held out a large hand to Carlos. Let me help you. You want to help? Carlos accepted his hand and rose to his feet. Is your support group over? Yeah, we wrapped about twenty minutes ago. Good. Then I need you to stay with Rosemary, the woman we brought to the hospital, until her son gets here. Should be about an hour or so. Can do. Carlos directed Don to Rosemary's location and raced out the ERs automatic doors. He hustled down the sidewalk. Nellie hadn't gotten far. He found her about fifty feet from the entrance, hugging a streetlight. How do you feel? He asked softly. Still a little dizzy? No, I'm holding this light because it's lonely. Oh, relly? This is the first time I've seen your sarcastic side. Put your head between your knees and take deep breaths. She did as he instructed. He rubbed her back lightly. After a minute she looked up at him. Just please tell me that wasn't Don with you when I came to. Tell me I was hallucinating. You want me to lie to you? Why does it matter? Her shoulders inched toward her ears, then dropped back down. I have to sit up. She straightened running a hand over her hair. The whisper of her sigh floated along the warm breeze. He waited.

Take me back to camp Carlos. She rose from the bench, digging in her pocket. He stood. The keys jingled as she passed them to him. Let's put the top down and ride with the wind in our hair and pretend we're young and foolish, without a care in the world. He folded her into his arms and held her tightly, offering comfort. He dropped a kiss on the top of her head, the tangy, lemony scent of her skin and hair stirring feelings of protectiveness in him. We can do that. And he could pretend it was all about sex. And forget the fact that he was starting to really care about this brave and vulnerable woman. The wind rubbled his hair as he guided the goat along the back country road. The engine's purr registered only vaguely in his mind. The full moon offered it's light from a cloudless sky filled with stars. Nellie tugged the ponytail holder from her hair, letting it fly free. The brown strands whipped around her face. That's better. Are you ready to talk about what happened in the hospital? She turned sideways in the seat as far as her seat belt would allow. Her index and middle fingers pressed gently on his lips. Not a care in the world, Carlos, remember? And I've told you what happens when you deny and suppress, remember? He kissed her fingertips to buffer the sting of his words. I thought you were my friend I am your friend. And friends talk about things that trouble them. They worked together to put the convertible's top up. Carlos circled around the car to her side. Nellie, I'm sorry things didn't go better. Not exactly what I had in mind for our date. Me, neither. She tipped her head back and looked up at him. But the night's not over yet. I was thinking about taking a walk down by the lake. Would you like to come? His fingers brushed over her hair. Yes I would. Okay. Just let me get something. She opened the trunk. An old comforter one she and Daniel had often used for picnics and a flashlight lay in the corner. Nellie pulled them out, clicking the light on. I found a wonderful place. Follow me, but watch your step. There are a lot of rocks and roots in the path. The moon added its glow, filtering down through the gently swaying trees. Weeds and tall grass covered what had once been a viable path; law shubs encroached along the edges. Nellie picked her way along the route. It led to a small, manmade beach along a secluded cove, tucked away from the main part of the lake. Nellie loved the spot and had come here several times. Here we are. She spread out the comforter on the sand, then sank down on it. What do you think? Carlos lowered himself beside her. How did you find this? It's great. On one of my early morning walks. She tipped her head back. Just look at all those stars. Carlos shifted until he sat behind her, his legs surrounding hers, arm enfolding her waist. How's that? With a contented sigh, she relaxed, molding her body against his, allowing her head to rest against his shoulder. Its nice, she murmured. Very nice. Mmm, I think so, to. The companionable silence was broken only by a breeze gently fanned her loose hair. Nellie snuggled deeper in to the warmth of the man who held her so tenderly. Fireflies flickered in the shrubs and grassed surrounding their private spot. Rose would have a field day with all these fireflies, she said. Probably. Carlos nuzzled her hair. Nellie tipped her head again and studied the heavens. Doesn't nature make you feel small and insignificant? Small and insignificant? Not really. I realized something tonight, she said finally. What's that? Life's short. Its just a blip in the grand scheme of things. He hand swept across the air. Just a blip. I realized that if there are things you want in life, you shouldn't put them off, you should go ahead and do them. I mean, Daniel she sighed, Daniel wanted to get on a big yellow school bus and go to kindergarten. There's no way I could have speeded that up for him. But take henry and Rosemary. Maybe they've alway's wanted to go to Europe but kept putting it off. Tonight, they almost ran out of chances. He cupped her face with his hand, thumb lightly caressing her cheekbone. And what is it you want before you run out of chance's, sweet Nellie. Heat Rose beneath the skin he stroked, spreading across her face. And down her body. She swallowed hard, then took the plunge. You, she whispered. I want you. He closed his eyes. Nellie, I...A sharp pain radiated across her chest, into her stomach. Had she mis read him earlier? Don't you feel the same way? His eyes flashed open. I want you, Nellie its just...What? I can't promise you a future, and you deserve someone who can give you that kind of security. Oh, Carlos. That's the first time anyone has put my needs first. And I mean it. He dipped his head, barely brushing his lips over hers. She closed her eyes and angled her head, waiting to feel his mouth on hers. Suddenly his hand left her face. Startled, she opened her eyes to see him jump to his feet. Carlos, wait! She leapt up as well. Don't go. Nellie, I'm sorry. But if I stay here, I'm going to do something you might regret in the morning. Something like make love to me? Like I want you to? She didn't wait for his answer. Life was too short, and Carlos was a very special man. She stepped close to him and flattened her palms against his chest. I'm not asking for forever, Carlos. I'm not even asking for tomorrow. I'm interested in right now, tonight. This moment may well be all we ever have, but I'm not willing to let it go by. She slipped her hands between his elbows and torso, wrapping her arms around his waist. Are you? She let her fingers explore the broad planes of his back. Could she seduce him? That was something else she'd never done. Throwing caution into the lake, she trailed her right hand lower, caressed the firm curve of his behind. Carlos inhaled sharply. His lips moved forward pressing his erection against her belly. Nellie...She lifted her fingers to his lips, but, if you really don't want to...She crossed to the center of the comforter, kicking off her sandals. Her fingers opened the top two buttons of her blouse. What are you doing? Well, I've never gone skinny dipping. And I think that's one of those things that should definitely be experienced in life, don't you? The moon light caressed her bare shoulders as she slowly lowered the garment. Carlos wanted to be that moonbeam, sliding across her satiny skin. A lacy bra cupped her small breasts. She tossed the blouse to the edge of the comforter and lowered her hand to the button on her capres. He had to remind himself to breath. The rasp of the zipper teeth echoed loudly in the little cove. She shimmied the tight denim over her hips, turning around to give him a full view of that perfect backside as the pants dropped to her feet. Oh, god. A thong. The woman actually wore a tiny, sexy, satin thong. Nellie...He barely recognized his own voice, it was so raspy and thick. She turned back to face him, a vision in moonlight and skimpy lingeree. Something wrong? Yeah. You take my breath away. She dipped her head, a sky smile on her lips. Two quick strides brought him to her. He cradled her face in his hands. You're absolutely sure about this? She nodded. He lowered his head and kissed her. Hard. Sweet butterscotch, warm woman...He slid his hands around her back, trailing down her smooth skin. The strings of her thong guided him lower, and he lightly ran his fingers over her curves. He tucked his hands around the silken flesh, pulled her against him. Her tiny shudder and moad deepened his desire. He trailed kisses down her neck, lingering in the hollow of her throat. Her hands pulled frantically at his shirt, I want to feel you against me. He yanked it over his head and dropped it to the ground. This, too, he said, reaching behind her to struggle with the clasp of her bra. His out of practice fingers fumbled until the fabric gave way. He slid the straps down her arms and tossed the garment aside, too. She pressed against him, the hard tips of her breasts igniting flames of desire. He scooped her up and placed her on the blanket, propping himself on his elbow over her. She folded her arms over her chest, a flicker of apprehension in her eyes. Don't cover them, Nellie. He gently moved her arms, watching her face carefully. I want to look at you. They're...Beartiful, he pronounced. With one fingertip, he teased the nipple to attention. Small. She gasped as he cupped her breast in his palm. Perfect. Good things come in small packages. I'd like to know your reaction if I say that when you drop your pants. Laughter erupted from deep in his belly. Aah, Nellie. You do make me feel young and foolish, like I haven't a care in the world. He leaned over to nibble on her earlobe, then whispered, but I don't think ill disappoint you. She smiled and caressed him through his jeans. Me, neither. He groaned and grabbed her wrist in a viselike grip. Honey, I've ached all night over you. It's been such a long time for me, and all I want to do is bury myself deep inside you. You touch me like that and the fireworks will be over before we even get started. She flexed her fingers, teasing him with a light touch even while he still

held her hand. Really? His turn to grasp. Really. Wicked...
sexy...woman. Only with you, she whispered. You make
me feel that way. Your husband was an idiot. She giggled
and stroked him again. He lowered his head and hesitated,
his warm mouth poised just over her breast, just out of
reach, teasing, tormenting. Two can play like that. He
circled her nipple with the tip of his tongue, making her
moan. Why don't you tell me the pleasurable image you
pictured back in the restaurant? The pleasurable? The one
that made you flush so nicely and catch your breath? She
ran her fingers through his hair. Oh uh, you're on the
right...right track. He lifted his head and grinned at her.
Really? Let me see if I can follow the track correctly. He
showered her body with kisses, starting between her
breasts and trailing lower. She sucked in her breath when
he kissed her navel, then circled it with his tongue, but
stopped breathing completely when he probed just under
the elastic of her thong. Don't hold your breath, Nellie. I
don't want you fainting again. It's tough on the male ego
durning sex unless you wait until your climax. Then by
all means, go ahead. He winked. Grinning up at her from
between her thighs, he placed his mouth gently on her
panties. Nellie felt scorching heat rocket through her.
You–you don't have to...No, I don't have to. I want to. Lift
up. She raised her hips and he peeled the thong from her
body. She clutched at the comforter when he began to
lavish the attention of his mouth on her. Nimble fingers

joined the game, leaving her panting when they teased and retreated. She scrunched her eyes shut. His elbow trembled with the exertion of holding himself over her. He kissed her thoroughly then dropped down beside her, rolled onto his back, and gathered her into his arms. Their ragged breathing slowly evened out and the roaring in her ears gave way to the sounds of the night; the wind in the trees and the frog chorus. Carlos tugged edges of the comforter around them and his hand nestle the top of her head. That was incredible. Will you tell me more about Daniel? Like what? Like, what was his favorite color? TV show? Did he sleep with a night light or was he a tough guy? Voice soft, she talked about her son, his love for yellow and vehicles of all shapes and sizes, his teddy bear, and his night light. He always had a smile for everyone. I wish to make love to you again. She pressed her belly harder against his erection. Tell me something I don't know. She smiled at him okay, did you know that this time, I'd like to do it in a bed? He groamed and reached beneath his side. I think I'm lying on a rock. She chuckled. All right. My place or your's? Your's is closer. He kissed the tip of her nose. I'll race you there. Race? Aren't you worried we won't make it there that we'll fall and get hurt? He threw the comforter off them and reached for his clothes. I'm more worried we wont' make it there fast enough, and ill end up grabbing you and making love to you in front of the cabins. His thought's turned to his daughter. Rose didn't deserve to be relegated to second place. It wan't her fault she needed so much of his time. And he wouldn't change her for anything. He loved her exactly the way she was. His pace slowed, and the gap between Nellie and him lengthened. Amazing how much clearer he could think when she wasn't close. When he walked up the creaky steps and onto her porch, she was already waiting, cabin door open, he followed her inside and dumped the comforter onto a chair. Our nights over already, huh? Disappointment was evident in her brown eyes. He shook his head. Not over just temporarily interrupted. I need to check on her. I understand. I figured you would. He strode to the cabin phone, then checked the time.

Only 10:42. Eddie would still be awake: he was a notorious night owl. I'll just freshen up while you make your call, Nellie said, heading for the bathroom. He waved her off. The phone rang only once, then Eddie's voice came across the line. Hello? Hey. It's me. Who else would it be? She's fine. I dragged her and Cherry into the cabin about thirty minutes ago, and they're settle in for the night. Go make use of those things I gave you and stop worrying. Worrying comes naturally. Are you sure she's okay? Listen, she's tucked into bed, snug as a bug in a rug. They're both probably sound asleep by now. A raucous burst of little girl shriek from the background nixed that idea. What's going on? Should I come down and get her? Pattering feet, and mumurs about shadows and monkey paws and something he didn't catch crept across the phone lines. Giggles followed, reasuring him. No, it's just these two are determined to keep me from my date with my wife. Hey, bud. It's only one night. Carlos laughed. I have no desire to follow in your chaste footsteps. Now hang up and turn your attention back to that pretty lady you're with. You are still with her right? He glanced at the closed bathroom door. The sound of running water came from the other side. Tell Rose I love her. Will do. Night, jimbo. Father responsibilities complete, Carlos hang up and turned his attention back to the bathroom door. He shed his shirt, draping it over the coffee table. Friday night was still young and for this night, so was he. Young, foolish, and with his cares tucked safely in bed, in the capable hands of his friends. He pushed the bathroom door open a crack. Steam rushed out. Nellie? You up for some company in there? Water streamed down her face as she peeled around the rainbow covered shower curtain. I thought you'd never ask. She chucked. I thought you'd find this a better idea than skinny dipping in the lake. Fewer germs. Hmm, you may be right about that. Maybe I should climb in there and make sure you don't miss any. Full body search for germs. She crooked a finger at him. So what are you waiting for? Lose those pant's and come on in. He eagerly accepted her invitation. The next day Carlos invited Nellie to go with him and Rose to a little amusement park a few miles away from camp. And when Carlos went to the bathroom Nellie took Rose on a small roller coaster without Carlos permission. And he was very upset because on the way home Rose got sick and he had to pull over and let her throw up. Carlos snapped at Nellie and they got Rose back to the cabin and into bed, that's when Rose told him that it wasn't Miss Nellie's fault that she found all of her snacks, and that's what made her sick on her stomock. Carlos said now try to get some rest Rose turned to her side. Then Carlos left and went into the living room where Nellie was waiting on him. I know you didn't mean to undermine my authority today. I'm sorry I even said that. It's just...Well, for one thing, I'm not used to having anyone else make decisions where Rose's is concerned. Nellie gave him a weak smile if I were writing your report card, I'd have to put doesn't share well with others; huh I guess. He shrugged. She's my life, Nellie. After being around all these other transplant parent's for a week, I'm starting to see that maybe I'm a bit overprotective. A bit? Her smile widened. Allright maybe a little more than a bit. But I almost lost her. And the idea of that, it...scares the hell out of me. So I'm forgiven? He brushed his fingertips over her shoulder. There's nothing to forgive. You're a concerned dad, that's all. I've waited all day for this, he whispered, leaning forward and pressing his mouth to hers for a brief kiss. Carlos was loving the way she made him feel. Carefree, alive, very much a man...

One more week with her was not going to be enough. The next day come on in. Don swung the door to his office wide and offered a sweep of his arm invitation. Nellie surreptitiously wiped her palms across the hem of her shirt as she entered. Don's office was larger than Trudy's featuring more than just the standard desk and filing cabinet. A sofa and armchair occupied one corner, and there was a large table with four hard backed chairs around it. And he had an air conditioner, for which she was very grateful. Maybe her hands would stop sweating. Don dropped himself into the armchair leaving her no option but to sit on the couch. Hard to believe two weeks had passed since she'd arrived. The hours she spent with Carlos had made time fly. Early morning walks with him and Rose, evenings spent around the campfire behind his cain. An occasional touch, a few stolen kissed. Though they hadn't made love again, Nellie treasured what they'd shared. So Nellie, tell me, has camp firefly wishes done anything for you? Okay, this was it. Her last chance to influence the report Don would undoubtedly be writing in the next few days. She nodded her head. I think so. What? Well, meeting these kid's has made me the next word's caught in her throat and she had to force them out glad that I agreed to donate Daniel's organ's. What else? She lifted both shoulders. I don't know. It's reminded me that life is for living, and I should get on with doing that. No matter how hard it is. Good. They talked about the kid's in her care, and the responses of the parent's to her, about her performance as the arts and craft's teacher. Don skirted around the issue of her relationship with Carlos and Rose. The camp director must have noticed something going on between them, but Nellie appreciated the fact that he didn't seem interested in discussing it. Let's talk about the night in the hopital. All the moisture from her mouth fled to her hands, causing a new round of sweating. She picked at a seam on the sofas cushion. I'd rather not. I'd like to know what you were thinking, what you were feeling that led up to your collapse, Nellie. Don's pen poised over the pad. In an instant, she could smell the disinfectants; hear the sounds, of the sirens and the babble of nurse's, see Daniel in that bed, all hooked up to monitors. No! She surged to her feet. I am not talking about that, I am not thinking about that! Easy. We're just talking here. Talking can't hurt you. Don rose, hand outstretched. No I'm leaving. Enough is enough. You'll have to write your report however you see fit, but I'm not talking about this with you. Or anyone else! She rushed out the door, the muggy air in the hallway making it hard to breathe, her first impulse was to run to car low. In his company she could forget about the bad stuff, the painful stuff. But what was the point in that? Tomorrow they were both leaving camp, he to Branford Fields, in the southwest corner of Pennsylvania, she to Elsworth, in the northwest corner. And that would be the end of it. Now was the time to stand on her on her own two feet. She pinched the bridge of her nose, hard. Sometimes life was a bitch. But a good soldier laced her boot's tighter and carried on. The camp's closing ceremony was just about over, and so was their time together. And he didn't like that idea one bit. And so, we extinguish the memory torch until next year, but we'll carry in our heart's the memorie's of the people we've loved and lost, and the memories of the people who made such a difference for others, giving life in a time of loss. Don solemn vaice ichoed over the crowd as he snuffed out the flam on top the rainbow colored torch. Black smoke drifted upward in the night sky. We hope to see a lot of you again next year. May you all be happy. And healthy between now and then. Carlos Carlos captured Nellie's hand as it headed for her face. He wove their finger's together and squeezed, knowing Don's words had stirred memorie's of her little boy. Darn! I can't believe camp is over already. Rose complained from his other side. Now we gotta go back home, and the rest of the summer is going to be boring I wanna stay longer. So did Carlos. He wasn't ready to give up on Nellie, on feeling like a more complete human being than he had in ages. Their stolen mement's over the past week had been welcome oases in his life. She'd pushed him to try things with Rose. A trail ride on horseback, a trip on the lake... But it was some of the other times he'd miss more. Her watching him tuck Rose in at night, his pulling her onto the porch where they'd talked and kissed like a couple of teenagers. But all that was over. He stifled the urge. To sigh. Sorry, tiger. That's the way it goe's. Before you know it, school will be back in session. Oh, great. I can hardly wait. Nellie chuckled. The crowed slowly diaspersed, making it's way off the beach, wandering back in the direction of the individual cabin's. Eddie clap Carlos on the shoulder. Well, jimbo, I guess that's about it for our vacations, back to work on Monday. How about one last compfire at your place? Please, Dad, please? Rose clasped her hand's together in supplication. Just one more hight? We can catch some more fireflies, and tell more stories. Roast a few more marshmallows, Cherry put in. After tonight, I won't get to see Rose again for a long time. Please? Carlos pretended to consider it for a moment, when the truth was, he was as eager as they were to prolong the experience. Okay. The girl's shrieked and jumped up and down. We'll meet you there! Rose grabbed Cherry by the hand and the pair took off down the road, weaving around other group's of campers. You'll join us, right? He asked Nellie. I should pack. I planned an early stat tomorrow morning. Like she was really looking forward to getting back home to her emty house...her empy life. Even her cat wouldn't be glad to see her diamond was probably miffed at being left with Mrs. Whitney for so long. And what would Nellie do for the next few weeks, until it was time to get ready for school?

Sit around and watch the paint peel? She realized that was exactly what she been doing since Daniel had died. Zoning out. Avoiding every one and anyone. Eddie had taken the girl's off to catch fireflies one last time. The wind rustled the top's of the tree's and swirled the smoke from the fire, lifting tiny red embers into the air. All that and more. He smiled. Let Michelle make of that what she wanted. So I noticed. There's been a certain spring in your step the past week. She settled the now sleeping infant into his carrying seat, then tucked a lightweight blanket around him. I hate to admit it, but it looks good on you what looks good on me? He glanced down at the shirt he wore, a yellow colored polo. Not your shirt, nitwit. Nellie. Nellie? He raised his eyebrows as Michelle sank into the lawn chair. I thought you didn't approve of me and Nellie? She has too much baggage, I believe you said. Or is it that you can approve now that camp's just about over? I worried, and I shouldn't have. She's been really good with the kid's. Michelle cocked her head as Eddie's booming laughter echoed from the front of the cabin. She broke into an easy grin. It's not good. To be alone, Carlos. I was concerned about the effect's Nellie's...loss...could have on you and Rose, I was wrong. Carlos slapped his hand across his chest. Write this down in the record book's. Michelle was wrong. Smart ass. So, you gonna keep seeing her? I checked out a map on the internet yesterday and Branford Fields is only about a two hour drive or so from Elsworth.

Weekends would be easily doabled. Weekend's. With Nellie. The thought appealed to him. And he'd already checked out the distance between their respective small towns. Definitely doable. I don't know, Michelle. What if Rose start's to read too much into the relationship? I'd hate to see her get hurt. Or Nellie. The memory of her collapsing in the hospital flashed by. Or me. Carlos leaned back in the chair, stretching his legs out and crossing them at the ankle's. He laced his finger's together and cupped his head in his palm's. Cricket's chirped, competing with the occasional throaty??? long the lake's edge. The wood smoke smelled pleasant. I don't even know if she'd want to keep seeing me, Michelle. For all I know, she's fine with the whole summer romance thing we originally agreed to. You'll never know if you don't ask. For once in your life, take a risk, Carlos. The sound of little girl giggle's drifted around the cabin followed by Eddie's mock roar, and then, high pitched shrief's. Michelle laughed. Maybe you'll get as luck as I did. A few trial weekend's. He and Rose could visit Nellie's house, she could stay with them. In the guessroom. He wouldn't give the wrong impression to Rose even if they were sleeping together, they weren't going to be sleeping together." He leapt from the chair and bolted in the direction of Nellie's cabin hoping to catch her before she even finished packing. And hoping she'd agree to keep seeing him. Be right back! Keep an eye on Rose for me! Carlos! Michelle yelled after him him don't run in the dark. You'll fall! Quite possibly. And the thought didn't scare him as much as he'd expected. He slowed to a trot outside her cabin, vaulted up the steps and onto her porch. He rapped on the door, then opened it. Nellie? In the bedroom. Come on in, Carlos. He found her packing again, though this time she was more organized. Her dresser didn't look as if it had exploded. She turned from placing something into her suitcase and offered him a slight smile. Did you bring me more fireflies? He shook his head. No. But I brought you something else. Oh? He crooked his fingers at her from the doorway. Come over here. When she was close enough, he reached out and pulled her into his arm's. She tipped her head, looking up at him. Closing the space between them slowly, he leaned forward and eased his lip's against her's. For several minute's they kissed, her hand's fastened tightly on the point's of his collar as she held him near finally he rested his forehead against her's. Ah, sweet Nellie. Aby regret's? No she said softly. Well just one. She smiled at him. What's that? I wish we'd had another chance she broke eye contact and her cheeks flushed to make love. He ran his fingers along her back. So do I. Maybe we can do something about it. Isn't everyone waiting at the campfire? I'm not talking about right now. He lifted his head from hers and took her hands in his. Nellie, two weeks isn't enough. I want more than this. I was hoping you'd agree to see me on weekends in the future. Weekends? Yes we could take turn's. On weekend's you come to my place, one weekend Rose and I come to your's. He searched her eye's for a hint of reaction as she stared at him. Well? A broad smile broke across her face and she nodded. I think that sound's like a fantastic idea. Her finger's tightened around his. Great, he said, lowering his mouth toward her's again. Then tonight isn't goodbye, it's just see you soon. Rose had been bored ever since camp had ended two week's ago. Okay. Gram had taken her to the movie's and grandpa had played video games with her, but compared to camp firefly wishe's all that was snore city. At least now things were looking up. This is it? She asked, bouncing on the back seat as her dad turned into the driveway. She peered through the gathering darkness, trying to make out the color of the building. This was too cool. They were spending the weekend with Miss Nellie. At her house! Cherry had assured her via e mail that this was a good sign. Maybe she'd get a new mom plan would be a success. Rose crossed her fingers. She'd just have to keep encouraging things. Yep, this is it. Dad ease'd to a stop. Rose already had one hand on the door, the other on the seat belt release. Hold it. I want you to remember all the thing's we talked about. Good manner's, good behavior, all that? Rose rolled her eye's. Like she'd forgot to make a good impression on the woman she wanted for a mom? Yes, dad. You remember your promise, too, right? No calling me unsinkable and absolutely no disinfecting.

You left the spray at home, right? You'll make Miss Nellie feel bad if you do that at her house." And Rose didn't want that. No matter what, she'd be sure her dad made a good good impression this weekend, too. The front door of the duplex opened and the light on the porch flicked on. Miss Nellie stood framed in the right. Hand doorway. She waved at them. Rose grabbed her backpack and tumbled out of the SUV. Dad followed, going around to the back to grab his bag. She raced up the steep porch stairs. Hi Miss Nellie. We're here! She smiled. So I see. Sorry we're so late. I had appointment's tonight. And one quasi emergency. Dad said. Not a problem. I'm glad you could make it. Come on in. She ushered them inside, right into the living room. Miss Nellie's house was tiny compared to??? Two archways opened in the opposite wall, one going into a dining room, and the other had a couple of step's up to a little landing. The smell of something yummy drifted through the air. A calico cat jumped off the back of the sofa and whisked past Rose's feet, darting up the stair's. Cool! You have a cat. A funny, strangling noise gurgled low in her father's throat and Rose knew what he was thinking. Cat boxes. Germs. That's Diamond. She's not big on people, so don't take it personally. What smell's so good? Rose tossed her backpack onto the cough and sniffed the air again I'm making a cake. Miss Nellie turned toward dad and made an apologetic face. I hope you don't mind, but there's a picnic tomorrow afternoon at my father's house. My brother Sloan, is visiting with his two girl's, and dad decided it was a good opportunity for a family get together. We don't have to go if you don't want, but I thought maybe Rose would like the chance to play with my nieces. That's fine. I'd like to meet the man who scared your hair pulling first grade teacher. Carlos smiled at her. Seeing her family would go a long way toward satisfying the curiosity he still had, the desire to know everything about her. Nellie spent the next few minutes giving them a tour. The first floor held the living room, dining room and kitchen, with an enclosed porch that ran along the back of the house. The most interesting feature of the house was the steps. From the living room, there were two up to a little landing then if you went straight, two more back down into the kitchen, but if you turned left, you could climb to the second floor. Carlos and Rose had never seen any thing quite like it. This is where you'll be sleeping, Rose, Nellie said as they passed the bathroom at the top of the stairs. She opened a bedroom door and stepped inside. Daniel's room. And Carlos was willing to bet she hadn't changed a thing since her son's death. Yet there wasn't a speck of dust on any of the furniture. Either she'd cleaned for their arrival, or she kept the room spotless as a sort of memorial. Light blue walls, a bedspread and matching curtains covered with yellow dump trucks and bulldozers, a short bookshelf that held dozens of childrens books. The sight of the fisher price school bus on the top of the shelf kicked Carlos aquare in the chest. He remembered Daniel's wish??? to go to kindergarten on a big yellow bus. Carlos set Rose's backpack on the floor. Time for you to brush your teeth and get ready for bed. It's late, and it seems like Nellie has plans for us tomorrow. Okay, dad. Downstairs, something beeped. My cake. Nellie brushed past him come down when you have Rose settled. Ten minutes and four prelutsky poems later, he ambled down the kitchen steps. Passing the fridge, he noticed a painting hung with magnets a big yellow shape with four black blobs along the bottom. He didn't need the neat, perfectly formed teacher's printing across the top to know it was a school bus and created by Daniel. Nellie inverted a cake pan over a cooling rack. As she set it on the white countertop, he sidled up behind her and sniffed deeply. Smell's terrific. Chocolate cake. I'll make vanilla icing in the morning. I was talking about you. He pushed aside her ponytail, dropped his mouth to the back of her neck and nuzzled the soft skin there. Mmm I've waited two weeks to do that. And this. Turning her, flush against him, then kissed her properly. Nellie's muscle's relaxed. She allowed herself to get lost in the pleasant sensations of his lip's on her's, his finger's drifting along her spine. One part of her remained aware, listening for any signs that Rose was still up, but the rest of her let go and simply enjoyed the warmth of this man. When he broke the kiss, she smiled up at him. It was worth the wait. I think so, too. The phone rang. Nellie crossed the living room to her oak roll top desk on the far side. She peered down at the caller id and cursed, something far stronger than her usual sugar cookies. What's wrong? Carlos asked, rising from the sofa. It's Peter. She grabbed the cordless receiver from the cradle. Dammit, Peter, I don't want to talk to you, so quit calling me! Taffing the off button did nothing to placate her annoyance, so she slammed it back into the base. Carlos wrapped his arm's around her from behind. You're trembling. How many time's has he called since the night we went out for dinner? A couple. Usually hanup on my machin cause even if I'm here, I don't pick up. But I've had enough. Have you talked to the police, stalking isn't something to be taken lightly. Stalking? She wriggled from his embrace and turned to face him. He's not stalking me. Peter isn't like that. An annoying pain in the ass, yes a stalker, no. He'd never hurt me or anything. Then what does he want? Don't know. Jerry said Peter just need's to talk to me. Maybe he's trying to come to term's with Daniel's death too? Looking for some closure? He stroked her cheek. Closure? Was that really possible when you'd lost such an important part of your life? Nellie shrugged, as much in answer to her own unasked question as to Carlos. I don't know. It's not my problem, is it? I'm busy enough trying to get myself together without worrying about him. Well, I'm worried about you. If he does seem unbalanced or if he doesn't get the message and stop calling, promise me you'll contact the police? Using her index finger, she rubbed gently at the tension lines in his face. Stop worrying. I'll be fine. The clock softly chimed eleven. It's late. Since you've insisted in sleeping down here on the sofa bed Carlos groaned. Nellie, I'd love nothing more than to share your bed upstairs, but not with Rose in the house. She pressed her lip's briefly against his mouth. I know, and I understand. Understood, but she didn't like it. The idea of spending the whole night in his arms was not only erotic, but strangely comforting. I was just teasing you. I'll be back with some pillow's. I put clean sheets and blankets on the bed this after noon. When she returned with his sleeping supplies. She paused on the landing enjoying the view as he smoothed out the beding on the sofa. He straightened up and turned. Catching her watching him. She dropped the pillows on the end of the bed, crooked her finger. Give me something to think about all night, cause I doubt I will be sleeping, knowing you're down here. The kiss he gave her definitely qualified as something to think about. Dream about. What are your intentions toward my daughter? Dean bush pointed a metal spatula at Carlos chest, brandishing the cooking tool in a confident manner that implied he expected a satisfactory answer. Burgers sizzled on the grill, their pleasant aroma filling this little corner of Dean's backyard. Carlos realized that being asked to help cook meant a grilling for him, as well as the food. His silver white hair in a short buzzy cut, and still fit and trim with muscular shoulders, the Sarge reminded Carlos of Richard Dean Anderson from Stargate. Sir? The respect came automatically. Hell, Nellie's father carried himself in such a way that you couldn't help but want to snap to attention and salute. No wonder she'd kept so much emotion hidden in order to please this man. You have a daughter, Carlos. I'm sure you can understand a father's desire to protect his little girl. Genuine concern filled the man's hazel eye's, then was quickly replaced with a stern expression designed to intimedate. Not that it did. The psychologist in Carlos had this man's number. He loved his daughter tremendously, and this was his way of showing it. I can understand wanting to protect your child, yes. Good. Because my daughter's been through a lot lately, and I'd hate to see her hurt again. Dean's jaw set in a firm line, and he returned his attention to the burgers. I have no intention of hurting her sir." No one ever does. Where's Nellie? Sloan, Nellie's older brother, trotted up onto the brick patio, face lined with tension. He had darker hair than his sister, but they shared the same hazel brown eyes. And right now, they were sparking with mixed anger and anxiety. I think she's in the house with Rose and Ashley, putting the finishing touches on the cake. Why? Carlos asked. Because Peter just drove up. Dean cursed and shoved the spatula into Carlos hand's. I'll take care of this.

He briskly strode from the patio, Sloan on his heel's. Carlos slapped the metal tool onto the redwood picnic table and raced after the other men. Did they know Peter had been hassling Nellie? He darted around Sloan's four door pickup with Texas plates and pulled up short at the driver's door of the goat. The two bush men stood near the front bumper, arm's folded across their chest's. Between father and son, there was enough muscle and testosterone to more than take care of one husband. Sarge. Sloan. Peter removed his wraparound sunglasses and slipped them into the pocket of his suit jacket. With his shoulder length dark hair neatly pulled back into a short ponytail, the man was not what Carlos had expected. He he had a bad boy aura that didn't match with the sweet image of Nellie. No wonder her father had wanted to know Carlos intentions. This man was the total antithesis of Nellie. Carlos moved forward to stand at Dean's other shoulder. Peter held out his hands. Look, guy's, I don't want any trouble. I'm just here to talk to Nellie. Five minutes, that's all I need. You've got five seconds to get your ass out of here before I kick the shit out of it. Dean popped his knuckles, either in warning or preparation. Sloan rolled his neck. I don't think my sister has anything to say to you anymore, Peter. A taunt squealed to a halt at the curb. The front door popped open, and a man with a rolling gait, more of a hobble than a limp, rushed toward them. Peter! What the hell are you doing? The dark man turned. Trying to talk to Nellie, Uncle Jer, just like you told me to. Here? Do you have a death wish or are you just plain crazy? Peter shook his head. Neither. Forget it. He yanked his sunglasses back out of his pocket and jammed them on his face. I've got a business meeting out of town. I'll be gone for a few days. I'll call you when I get back. He started toward his charcoal Lincoln town car. He pulled away from the curb and took off at high speed. You gotta do something about him, Jerry, or I'm going to, Dean said. He really needs to talk to her, sarge. I swear to you, I have Nellie's best interests at heart. You know I love her, too. I wouldn't BS you." Does this have anything to do with Daniel? Carlos asked. They all turned to look at him as though he'd appeared out of nowhere. Dean shook his head. I don't give a damn what it has to do with. I will not allow that man to upset my daughter any further, Sloan and Jerry nodded. After a moment, Carlos did, too. Nellie's father was not a man to be argued with. But the psychologist in Carlos couldn't help thinking that comforting Peter might be good for Nellie, especially if she could do it where her family and Carlos could support and protect her. Rose watched Ashley bush apply make up, torn between envy and horror. Green eye shadow and the black lipstick...Yuck. Did it hurt a lot to get your eyebrow pierced? Of course it did. The girl globbed on mascara. So what'd you do it? The thirteen year old laid the tube on the dresser and glanced at Rose in the mirror.

To get my father's attention. Did Rose and Ashley had quickly discovered a common bond the lack of a mother. Ashley's mother had been killed in a car accident three year's ago. She and her little sister, who was only four now, lived in Texas. With their father. Do you wish you had a mother? Rose rolled over onto her stomach on the double bed in the small but tidy guest room. Propping her chin on her palms, she kicked her feet in the air. Hellno. What would I want another mother for? I want one. I'm hoping miss Nellie can be my new mom, you know what my father says? Ashley whirled to face her. Rose shook her head. Be careful what you wish for. You just might get it. So? Why should I be upset if I get Miss Nellie for a mom? I like her. She's cool." Ashley's laugh was sharp. Mental case is more like it. Besides, you don't want to be part of our family. We tend to lose people. My grandma, my mother, my cousin, Daniel...Were hard on family around here it's a curse. That's just stupid. Sometimes people die. That's right, tiger. Sometime's they do, her dad said softly from the doorway. And it hurts. But we have to keep moving forward. You need to wash up. Rose scrambled from the bed, hoping her dad hadn't overhead the start of that conversation. He wasn't supposed to know that shed wished for Miss Nellie to be her new mom. Okay, dad. Your father said for you to come down, too, Ashley. Whatever. Ashley moved back to the dresser. I'll be there when I get there. Rose followed her father into the hall way, realizing that despite his stupid cleaning stuff, and all that, her dad was a pretty cool guy and she was lucky to have him. With Miss Nellie, they'd make a complete family. And everything would be perfect. Shrieks of childrens laughter rang across the backyard. Several of the neighborhood kids three boy's and a girl had come over. After a spoon and potato race, organized by Sloan, the group was now involved in a lively game of tag. Rose appeared to be having a great time. Ashley watched from the sideline, doing her best to appear nonchalant, but sometime's not able to keep the longing from her green shaded eyes. Carlos and Sloan had commiserated on how hard it was to raise girl's by themselves, and Nellie's brother had warned him that things only got worse, that the terrible teen's made the terrible two's look like a cakewalk. Sloan cradled his younger daughter against his chest, absentmineedly stroking her chestnut hair. All the adult's were slumped in lawn chairs on the edge of the patio. I still can't get over it, Jerry muttered. Over what? Nellie asked. The fact that little Rose has had a heart transplant. Jerry faced Carlos. I'd never have known. Thank's. She's doing great. Jerry leaned over and grasped Nellie's hand. See? Aren't you glad that you donated Daniel's organs? Somewhere out there are kids who can run and play today because of what you did. Yeah, Jer. I'm glad. Nellie gave his fingers a quick squeeze, then pulled her hand free. But she wasn't, nothing could ease the pain in her own heart, the wish that Daniel still ran through his grandfather's backyard with the neighbor kid's. She could feel her fathers intense gaze on her. She pinched the bridge of her nose. Rising from the chair, she headed for the picnic toble. I think I'll take a few of these things back into the house and put them away. The mustard bottle tipped over as she reached for the leftover potato salad. I'll help. Carlos followed her into the kitchen, arms laden with the condiment's and the cake. He plunked them down on the counter, removed the big plastic bowl from her arm's, and set that down, too he pulled her into an embrace: Are you okay? Fine, she mumbled again this chest, content to once again draw comfort from his strength. No, you're not. Every time you get upset, you do that thing with your nose. What thing? She tilted her head and looked at him. This thing. He gently pinched the upper postion of her nose. Nellie offered him a halfhearted smile. Busted. You're very observant, counselor. Is there anything I can do for you. Nellie? Actually, yes. Would you...I haven't been to Daniel's grave in a while, and I don't want to go alone. Would you go with me? His eye's widened, as if she'd knocked the breath right out of him. I uh never mind. No, no I'll go with you. It's just...What about Rose? I'd really rather not take her. She can stay here with the kids. My father and brother Sloan will watch her. We won't be gone long. The cemetery is only about ten minutes from here. Please? He exhaled deeply. Okay. Let's go. He followed her silently as they moved among the headstones. Birds chirped in the nearby tree's, and though the hot summer sun beat down on them, goose bump's Rose on Carlos arm's. Nellie stopped on front of a blue gray, roughly rectangular marble monument. The side's cushed, and a heart was hewn in the upper left corner. She stooped and threaded the ribbon's from the ballons through a slit in the stone along the bottom posrtion of the heart. Carlos began to squat beside her, but a small package in his pocket jabbed him in the thigh. He withdrew the purchase he'd made downtown from the little all purpose store while Nellie had been occupied with selecting Daniel's ballon's. Hey there, Daniel. In his mind's eye, he could see the smiling boy from the picture on her mantel. A lump swelled in his throat as the true impact of Nellie's loss stormed him. This child, her child, had been one whom laughed and loved, played and slept...and in his final rest, had given other's another chance at life. He cleared his throat and forced the words past his strangled vocal chords. I brought you somthing, buddy." He set the tiny yellow school bus on the monuments base. Oh, Carlos. He turned to look at her. Her lower lip quivered, and she covered her mouth with a trembling hand hand. Tears welled up in her eyes, but she made no attempt to stop them. They spilled over and trickled down her face. She rose to her feet. He stood and gathered her into his arms. I am so sorry, Nellie, he murmured into her hair. Sheltered against his chest, Nellie let the tear's flow. He'd brought Daniel a school bus. In that moment, she realized she loved him. Carlos. The man who'd taught her it was okay to cry. Who'd taught her what it was to live again. And she loved Rose, his courageous, spunky, hell of a kid. Nellie bit her lower lip in an effort to stem not the tear's, not the grief, but the sudden and overwhelming fear that followed the revelation she was in love with both father and child. She'd barely survived losing Daniel. Would she survive losing again? Rose's transplanted heart left her at risk. Hospital's. The word brought the cloying scent's and rush of further terror. Loving Rose and Carlos would automatically mean confronting hospital's and doctor's. Nellie wasn't sure she could do that. Several day's later, armed with a pair of empty cardboard boxe's and some strapping tape, Nellie paused in the entrance to Daniel's room, she set the supplie's on his bed then moved to his dresser, skimming her fingertip's over the over the oak leaves carved into the surface. She sighed, started with the bottom drawer, pulling out jeans, army sweatshirt given to Daniel by her father went into the to be saved box. Quickly and methodically, she made short work if the dresser. The cat brushed against Nellie's ankle. She bent and scooped her up, stroking the soft fur. I know, Diamond. It's weird, isn't it but we have to clean this up. I want to start the new school year looking forward. Diamond purred and rubbed her head against Nellie's chin. The sound of a car in the driveway came through the open bedroom window. She moved to brush aside the curtain. Damn Diamond still clutched against her chest, Nellie flew down the stair's and flung open the front door just as her ex husband climbed to the top of the porch steps. Peter. What the hell are you doing here? Peter held up his hand's. Nellie, please I just need five minute's of your time, then I'm out of your life for good. I thought you were out of my life for good after Daniel's funeral. The steel gray eye's darkened. He blinked quickly several times. Nell, I know you blame me for what happened to Daniel. Hell, most of the time. I've blame me. But it was an accident. I swear, I looked away for just a minute, so you could kiss the bimbo. Well...His face flushed. That's true. Believe me, if I could change it, I would. Why are you here? You didn't come here just to ask my forgiveness, did you? It's a little late for that Nellie lowered the squirming cat to the floor and stepped out onto the porch as Diamond took off toward the kitchen. Peter climbed the final step. I have something to tell you. I wanted to tell you myself. He leaned against the banister and stared at her. What have you been doing? You've got a big piece of tape stuck to your arm. He pointed. Nellie ripped the tape off without flinching, even though it yanked out about a million tiny hairs. Weakness would not be displayed in front of this man. If you must know, I was packing up some of Daniel's thing's." Peter's mouth opened, then closed. The tiny muscle on the of his jaw twitched. Are you getting rid of everything? She shook her head. Of course not. If you come across that baseball mitt I gave him for his birthday, id...Peter turned his head away from her, staring at the company furnished Lincoln in the driveway. I'd like to have it, he finished in a choked voice. Uh. Sure. She silently cursed the softening in her chest, the acknowledgement that Peter actually felt pain over losing Daniel. That had been her exclusive territory. But as Daniel's father he was as entitled to feel loss as she was. And Nellie should be relieved to discover that he did feel some thing. This was the man she'd initially been attracted to. The man who'd given her Daniel. I'll set set it aside for you when I find it. Thanks. For a few moment's they simply stood on the porch, listening to the wind rustle the leaves. Finally, Peter cleared his throat again and turned to face her. Nellie, I'm getting married again. To Clarissa. This weekend. Oh. Slowly his words sank in. There was a flash of anger over the fact that he was moving on, but it was short. She silently thanked Carlos for the fact that she felt no jealousy. He'd made her feel every inch a desirable woman. Well, thank's for telling me. He took another step toward her. That's not all of it. Quilt filled his face. She'd seen that look before. Oh. My god. From nowhere, a combat boot struck firmly in her gut as understanding downed. No, she whispered. Don't tell me she's pregnant. Peter inclined his head. I guess you didn't figure out not to buy your condoms here in town! She yelled. Don't learned from your mistakes, huh, Peter? Daniel wasn't a mistake, Nellie.

And this baby isn't either. Nellie searched the porch for something, anything, to hurl at his head, but came up empty. You bastard! You son of a bitch! She slumped against the front door for support. She'd been packing her baby's life into boxe's, and he'd been makeing another one. A black pickup truck roared right onto the front lawn, crushing the green blade's of grass. Her father jumped out of the passenger side, and sload swung down from the drivers. Side the troop's had arrived. And she'd never been happier to see her family. I though I told you to stay away from my daughter? Her father grabbed Peter by the shirt and dragged him down the stair's. Easy, Sarge. Peter regaind his balance, and again held his hand's up in a gesture of supplication. I told her what I needed to tell her. I'm going now. He turned back toward her. I'm sorry, Nellie. I never meant to hurt you. Nellie, her father and her brother watched, motionless, until Peter drove away. How did you know? Nellie asked. Sloan pointed at the opposite side of the duplex. Mrs. Smith called dad when she saw Peter pull in. Nellie waved her thank's to the landlady and friend, who nodded and dropped the curtain back in place. You okay, sis? Sloan gathered her into a hug. What the hell was so important he had to tell you in person? Nellie briefly squeezed her brother, then backed from his embrace. Her father watched her carefully. She pinched the bridge of her nose. Good soldier's didn't cry. Oh, not much just that he's getting married again. Her stomach churned. And having another baby." Why, that... Her father launched into a series of word's Nellie had learned early her dad could use, but she couldn't repeat. His hand's curled into fist's. You want us to flatten him for you, Nell? Sloan offered her a quick grin, but he wasn't teasing. She shook her head. He's not worth a jail sentence, that's for sure. Beside's she ran her finger's down Sloan's arm, desperate to connect with someone, aching from holding inside the whirlwind of emotion she wanted to let go in her own own way. Peter's hurting, too. I just didn't realize before now. The sound of the ringing phone came through the front door. I have to get that. Come in, guys. You want some lunch? No, thanks. Sloan said. If you're okay, we should run. We left the kid's alone. I know at thirteen Ashley should be able to watch her little sis for a few minute's, but these days. I just don't know what she's fixin to do next. Anxiety and tension showed in her brother eyes. How had she missed that before? Too busy with her own problem's to see those of the people around her, the people who mattered to her. She made a resolution to sit down with Sloan and have a long talk. Talking was good. Carlos said so. Oh, Carlos. Nellie's throat tighten as the impact of Peter's new's hit her again. Somehow she didn't think talking would be enough to ease this pain.

Yes Nellie had an affair with her psychologist. You have to understand that it was a very tender time for Nellie, she was going through so much loseing her son and husband. Which Daniel's death just crushed, her emotionlly some what physially also, everyday she drew from and further away from other people even her own relative's. So Nellie knew that she and Carlos could never be together with his daughter Rose and get married and be afamily, like they or the three of them dreamed of, so she explained the way she felt to Carlos and he explained to daughter Rose, of course Rose was upset about the whole thing because she wanted a mother desperately and wanted Nellie particular to fill those shoe's. Eventually they stoped visiting each other. But sometime Carlos would call just to see how Nellie was doing and Nellie would call to see how Carlos was doing. But the call's gradually stoped. Nellie heared like it was someone at the door, it was Bobby and she had not ran his bathwater yet, oh man she thought my memory is really comeing back to me ofcourse the doctor's said that she would start remembering. The thing's that she had suppressed and held back for so long every since she was a little girl at lease the thing's she assumed to be true. Of Nellie's greatest asset advantage was she had and still have is seeing exact pricisely, correct not adding or takeig from. Bobby walked in the door. Hi! Boy am I glad to be home it rain so hard, I allmost got rushed off the street coming down the over pass from the hospital. Thank god for takeing care of me, Nellie said wash your hand's and sit down and eat somthing it'll make you feel better. Then Nellie moved on to the bathroom to run Bobby's water so he could bath the work off, makebe watch a movie with her, or go to bed any way the wind blow will be good with Nellie so after Bobby took his bath they went to sleep just as soon as their heads hit the pillow. Next morning Nellie got up took her shower cooked breakfast, and got ready to go to bible study at the kingdom hall. At that time was located back out in the wood's not to far from the loop and thirteenth street, Nellie learned so much and they became like family. It was the family of the true god whom she prayed to all of her young life, to meet them, to get to know the truth about god and Jesus. Exactly where did they come from, why is things so bad like they are, if he's got the whole world in his hands, what happen to make it this way. Is there a end, and how can we be saved, and how long will it take. She learned all these thing's and more. The sister's and brother's were saving money to build a new kingdom hall on highway seventy nine across the street from Watson Chapel School, how exciting and wonderful. Nellie was still having her individual study's at home in the trailer house on Fifth Street. She was studying once a week, going to bible studys once in the morning on Tuesdays, and Sunday. Nellie use to talk on the phone with some of the sisters. There was one particular sister of faith name Bernice, whom she talked to and they would talk about how they lived there life before Jehovah god. And learning word his name, and his purpose for mankind. They talked about when both of them use to go out to nightclubs, and all the place's they would hang out at. Place's they shouldn't have been. They talked about how glad they are to be free in there mines. Although her only sister Liz lived next door, they had to talk on the phone a lot because she was ill and didn't have the energy to even walk next door. The doctor's hadn't found out what was wrong yet but they were taking all kind's of test's some they were taking over again. It took seem like for ever to Nellie but they didn't give up neither did Nellie. When they found out, she begain to take treatment's and felt a little better until this day. Of course she's older and feeling it too. Liz was studying with Nellie, and what she learned she taught her sister, and told her to teach the rest of her family if she could get there attention. I am sure that she did the best she could. But mostly everybody still believe that when you die you go to heaven or hell depending on how good you've been and how bad you've been. So it's allmost impossible to even show them what the bible say about such thing's they can see it and still not beleive. But the main things is to try to show them in the bible andnot to worry about nothing, but showing and explaining it to the best of your ablity and leaving it to them to decide what the bible is really saying. Because of what they've been taught all of there life by there relative's and relious leader's. Nellie would allway's make it back home in time to have lunch with Bobby and see him off to work. Before she start their dinner and do a little house work, maybe even take a nape, watch a little tv and meditate on what she had studied in the bible that day. She would try so hard but things would flood her mine from the past. The memory of Bobby came to mine, the time when she first saw him, he was with his friend Buddy Hinton, they worked at the same place name the Paper Mill. They worked on the outside of the foundery, in different kind's of machine's in which they used for I don't know what kind of work was done with those big complecated looking machines, some look like what a person would use on a farm. That particular day, Buddy had off of work, he liked my sister Liz so he cames over to my mothers house and at that time she was living and things were much happyer then. So Buddy was talking to my sister Loz, he asked her to go for a ride and ask me to come because his friend Bobby wanted to meet her sister Nellie. Because he had seen her at the club that Saturday night and he was impressed and wanted to meet her. Nellie had just gotten back from California, she went straight to her mother's house. Her mother was hiome as allway's. They were glad to see each other, Nellie headed to the kitchen to see if there was any thing to eat or cook because she felt like both of them could eat something at that time. She found a whole chicken, pototos and carrot's.

She begain to cut the chicken in peice's to wash and fry, she peeled the potato's and cut them into french fry's and then she peled and washed the carrot's and put them into a pot to boil down in low water then add butter and leave simmering until it look like gravy take off stove to cool and soon Nellie and her favorite mother were eating fryed chicken french oven frys and carrot's. They watched tv and enjoyed their home made meal, Nellie was just glad that she didn't have to go to the near by store walking to get something to eat for them after they finished she cleaned up and took a bath, she put on a white short sleeve blouse and a pair of jean short's. Nellie left her mother's house walking. She had to walk about four block's to get to a little club name Ed's place to see her sister and she really needed a drink so when she walked into the club her sister Liz recognized her right away and yelled her name Nellie you're back and hugged her how long this time Liz asked her, she said who know's a month or maybe two, how have you been doing sister? Good said Liz, Nellie and their brother's called Liz sister. Nellie really wanted Liz to leave with her but she had three little girl's at that time. The oldest child name Charleete was only 11 or 12 year's old, her second child name Charletta was about eight or nine year's old and last but not least her baby girl was six years old all of them in school, Nellie think's that was the only reason she didn't go with her to their cousin house in California. Liz allway's said when Nellie come ba to Pine Bluff, she seemed so happy and looked rested and beautiful. She was right Nellie felt so wonderful. That was one of those time's that Bobby saw her and kind of talked to her over to Ed's one Saturday night and someone she knew asked Nellie tell him about what was going on up in Calee and she was talking out loud about California and Chicago, where she visit off ten, she was sitting up at the bar drinking a beer, there was a baby face boy looking man at her right talking also and she was thinking to herself who is this person helping her describe the way things, and people were in Chicago. And later that week his friend Buddy picked Liz and Nellie up, and took them out to where they worked and interdunce them and Nellie became very angry and upset because Bobby was behind a fence doing something or some kind of work and he woulded say anything, only smileing and she looked hard and then walked away not because she thought he wasn't good enough, but she was not for sale and that meeting made her feel funny inside. About one month later throught dume and friend's, they begain talking on the phone and Bobby is a really nice considerate, understanding and loveing person. He use to help Nellie around the house. When she took sick and had to have surgery, which she was laid up for month's geting well. Nellie decided that Bobby was the right man for her because of how kind he was. He was so loveing and kind. He never talked about her family or put them down like a lot of haters did.

He was very kind, acceptable and blend into her family as a brother in law, should. He would hold Nellie in his arms with out sex because he felt her need for his strength. She had been through so much, loseing half of her family and her own child and her first marriage didn't work and she was left alone with nomoney, no job, nobody to help her. Only there word's. Help yourself, well sometime a person weak need's a little help, a little kindness, a little love showing. Not just saying to get up off the ground to start over to try living again. Doing for themselves, because you can get so low until there noway you can get up on your feet again alone. You have to be a stone pony to live in Pine Bluff. There are some people who know what that mean. For the one's who don't know. It just mean being tough, tough and tough. Bobby and Nellie was married in the court house in Pine Bluff Arkansas. They were so happy for the first time, for both of them. It had been a long time tryin to pull each other up out of the gutter. Trying to keep each others feeling's up, makeing sure one wasn't getting depressed, by going to the movies, when they could not really afford it. Goin out to eat no where fancy. Mcdonalds or taco bell, was a pure pleasure. Geting out of the house and he did not forget about his two boy's that he had with his ex wife Dorothy. He had the hospital where he worked to take child support out of his paycheck. And his exwife is remarried now. But now those two boy's are all grown. His oldest son whom Nellie call BJ Bobby

Jr. Is married and have a son name Christifur Addison, He is fifteen year's old now and he's in the Rotc at his school and after graduateing plans to continue his career in the air force. Chris call his grandpa regularly to see how we are doing and want's to come over to visit. But lately with the corona virus hiting so hard, he has not been able to come over for a while. I can remember when he use to come over on the weekend, he would help Nellie clean the fish bowl and that was a really big deal for Nellie because it was too biger deal for her alone and meant a lot to her because they would talk and bond. This was a good for her to cook all that old fashion homemade food that Bobby, Nellie and Chris would enjoy very much. But when he got to be a teenager. And you know how they change. The more Chris wanted to eat out. Well Nellie did to, because she was tired of cookin she's geting older so everything was all good with her. Only Bobby didn't like spending so much money, but it was cool because he really love doing what he can for the kids and grand. BJ Bobby's oldest son has a two year old daughter and his baby girl like all daddy's little girl's has him wrapped around her finger and everybody enjoy watching them play. She's talking now, saying some words real clear so maybe after this pandemic virus the whole family can spend time together like before. Hopefully they want change to much while their're apart. Iknow Nellie and Bobby seem to have changed. Their're older and feel it to, for one thing but it will be fun to get out of the house, to go to a movie, to a dance, or go to a blues show. Even have a family BBQ. Sometime it seem hard to get family together for these affairs. Nellie has not been able to fingure this out. Maybe they'll be ready to do family stuff since the we all had to stay at home. Maybe it's her imagination. She has decided that if they want to come over to make them feel welcome. One thing about Nellie is that she allway's want to please and make everybody feel confortable and just allway's looking out for everyone else beside's herself. But lately she's been thinking about her own happyness and security. Until she felt afraid, Bobby could careless, he's just a wonderful guy, loveing father, loveing neighbor, loveing nephew and loveing friend. Loving all American soldier, sociable person that Nellie just happen to love for being that kind of person. Bobby started to study the bible and go to the kingdom hall on Sunday's with Nellie. But like all people he thought that Jehovah's Witness was acult. But found out that it it is on the up and up. Believeing in calling God by his name and his son Jesus Christ. Nellie was so glad that he found this out for himself. Because she was geting tired of defending her faith. So she let Bobby go and see for himself and decide like everybody else do. When Nellie feel bad now, Bobby support and provide her with food, clothing, to help her pain. But most of the time of the time Nellie's condition is beyond the observable physical world. Bobby offten talk to Nellie about how he felt when he was fighting his way back up out of the bad situation he had found himself in again. And he told Nellie that at a young age of six year's old. He was working in the cotton fields back home where he grew up at with his mother because she didn't have a baby sitter and she had to take him to the fields with her with a crooker sack on his back that he would be putting cotton in to put in his mother's sack when he filled it. Then after he grew up he was still working on Mr. Earl Clemmon's farm in Tamo Arkansas. At the age of twelve, he was chapping cotton from seven am to seven pm everyday. At fifteen year's old he was driving tractors. And as he became a man. At twenty years old, he left the farm and inlisted into the army. He was a recovery specialist. Where he drove trucks haurling tank's. And he stayed from Aug. 11, 1978 to 1984, Their a toebar fell on his right foot and he had a problem wearing the combat boot's and his left foot and right foot got infected badly, and he had to have surgery on both left and right foot. Then he had to wear two cast on both feet, up to his knees. He wore the cast on both of his feet up to his knees for about about three months. Thank God it was very near his time to get out of the service. And go home. And he did in 1984, he did odd jobs in Pine Bluff, until he started working at the Jefferson Hospital. And worked his way to being superviser in house keeping. He stayed their for ten year's, and he started haveing trouble with his feets, both shoulder's and could not continue working this job which required a lot of walking and lifting. Then he applyed for his disability from the army and social security. And it took a while, year's and it was very hard times for Nellie and Bobby because she was just geting about four hundred a month. And when Bobby got his disability, Oh happy day. Because they had no one to go to for help. The Hospital tryed to keep him on as the best superviser they had, but he coulded do the work. So he walked away in 2001 with that title superviser. Then the phone rang, Nellie picked the phone up and it was Bobby makeing his second check on Nellie to see if she was allright. Nellie and Bobby decided to move from their little trailer house on Fifth Street to a nice three bedroom and two bath, living room very large rap around kitchen and dinning area bugallow brick house. They found the perfect little wonderful area off of Indian Hill onto Silver Fox Lane. This is where Bobby and Nellie have made there home for nine year's. Bobby's youngest son Jarome got married. Had two kids a boy that he and his wife name Blake and he's 11 years old they also have a two years old little girl whom they call Riley. Bobby's son's little girl's were born about a week apart, Riley was born in Texas and Bobby Jr. little girl Skylar was born in Pine Bluff Ark. Bobby and Nellie call her Sky. What a joy they are? Well you know how grand parant's are, they can't do no wrong. Grand kid's get away with more than there parant's did. Before the outbreak of the corona virus BJ and Solona use to use to bring the little two year old girl Sky over every other weekend for a visit and it was fun watching her play and BJ trying to keep her out of trouble. Nellie was planing to have a Bar BQ. But now they will just have to wait until this corona virus get better before we all can get together for that. Bobby and Nellie stay at home most of the time unless they need something from the grocery store. Which both of them glad its close to there house. Thank god for that because both of them have been suffering from their illness. I guess every one has there own special pain in the body. Doctors and the medicine they perscribe can help ease these problem's and exerise does help. But sometime's the pain can be excruciating, until your body get's use to it. Then it'll become easier, it's something to get use to because life is pain that can be made better. It really depend's on the person determination to achieve what ever their goal's are and accelerate o them. When Bobby and Nellie moved into there new home on Silver Fox, they had some new really nice furniture. And it just complemented the beautiful house which looked like new. All they needed to do was wash the wall's and shine the paneling part. Everything was in place perfectly. They lived in their home for four good year's. Then one evening Bobby's son Bobby Jr. called his father. And asked him to come and help him get his car stated so he could go to work. At first

Nellie decided to stay at home because she was so comfortable on the sofa watching tv, then Bobby asked her again are you sure that you want go and get a little fresh air, you haven't been out of the house in a couple of day's. We can stop and get us a sandwich on the way home because it want take long, so it did sound okay and she got up off the sofa and put on her coat and boot's and left with Bobby. And when they got over to BJ's place he was outside with the hood of his car up. Bobby pulled up and parked his car where he could give his son a boast, he was right it didn't take long at all. Bobby got in his car and he and Nellie left to let the boy go to work and started for home. Nellie told Bobby to go on home because she had allready cooked and their food was in the oven waiting for them. There was no reason to waste any money. And when they turned off Indiana Hill's to their street on Silver Fox. They could see their neighbor's standing outside looking at their house. It wasn't a big flame, mostly smoke and fire truck's. Bobby had to park the car at a neighbor's house and walk over to their house and talk to the fireman. It was a good thing that their pat dog name Precouse was outside and had ran back of the garage out of fear, where he felt safe. The fireman went behind the garage in dark, and picked him up to bring him to Bobby and Nellie's arm's. They could see that he was allright so the fireman told them to put the dog down in the back yard which was fenced. There was a man at the house from the red cross. He helped Nellie and Bobby get in a hotel room. It was okay except you couldn't get but one channel on the tv and it was so boring. And Nellie didn't sleep well at all. They had to stay there two night's. Bobby then got in touch with the insurance company and they got them another, better hotel room over by the Pines Mall. It was clean and didn't smell bad at all. Nellie could rest and take her medicine, the hotel served a good big breakfast and they had to buy lunch and dinner. Most of the time they would microwave lunch and dinner. They would eat some and put the left over's in a compack refrigerator to heat up when needed. It was sure better than the first two hotels they stayed in. The weeks Nellie and Bobby lived in this holtel, her best friend from childhood passed away, name Sally. That hurt Nellie and Liz, and the brothers LB, Robert and Floyd to their soul because she was there sister in every way but blood. But it seem like it. They were raised from baby's together. It hurts Nellie today and it's been five or six years ago, it may ease up some but it will ve never be completely unpainful until Jesus fix things, and we can educate ourselves by studieing the bible. But also realize that you must prepare for your death and seek knowledge that can lead to everlasting life for ourselves and out family and friends. Nellie knew that she was a good person but being good was not all it was going to take to get in the kingdom of god. She seeked more information from the bible. Her mother and father and all those old prayer meetings did not have the answer to. She had to know without a doubt the truth that leads to enternal life and she found it. But was not sure so she had to go on further until there was no doubt in her mind. Satan couldn't come with doubt, and making her have such doubt against god. The god that made life itself. This was not easy, this is the most difficult thing Nellie had ever had to do. To deny herself and what all the people taught her. It was true just mixed up from all the years. From different people seeing and preaching from their head instead of every word in the bible. Don't beleive me, but study the word for yourself and ask god to help you understand. You see Nellie wasn't wearing a halow. She made misstakes. Big misstakes. And there will be more, but try not to make the same ones over and over again. And when you make a misstake against god and realize it, ask for forgiveness and he'll forgive you and give you the courage to pick yourself up and dust off to go on with your life. And do the best that you can. There may be other times when she got coaught in satans traps because the flesh is weak. But you have to be on the watch for these traps and truely learn from all your mistakes at least don't keep on makeing the same ones. You see when Nellie had that affair with her therapist she didn't lose her oppertunity for everlasting life. She was wrong, realized it, stoped doing it. And went back to god humblely asking for his forgiveness. And she beleive that the creator of this world has forgiven her. And she's going on with her life with her husband Bobby, grand kid's and the rest of her family. When Nellie and Bobby did move back into there house on Silver Fox. They had to redecorate the house which its been a five years sence they been back home. And they are still decorateing their little home. The house is just not the same. But before the fire Nellie thought her house was perfect lookig from the front to back outside and inside. Twenty minutes later she was alone in the loving room drinking a glass of wine. And she started to remember when she and Bobby got engaged. It was one day when Bobby was house sitting at his friend house. And Nellie's brother in law Dennis, at that time was Liz husband. One day Nellie was over their talking to Bobby, telling him that they should get married before bore staying together because it wasn't right in gods eye's. Yeah. Well". He reached over and awkwardly took Nellie's hand in his. Were going to get engaged. Why don't I cook you dinner next Saturday evening to celebrate, she said as she moved toward the front door. Sure, sure, Bobby said. That'd be great. Bobby followed Nellie out. He caught her on the porch, his hand on her elbow. You're really okay with this? I promise. Okay if you're sure? He gave her another hug. Say there's something else, to. About this guy Carlos. I hear he's back. She nodded. You worried about it? Her need to talk to him about it, to find out what he thought she should do, surfaced. But this wasn't the time. Not with the kids here. Not as a follow up to their happy news. Bobby it was a long time ago. Bobby gave her a long, hard look. A skeptical look. You need anything you call, I'm right here, you know little girl. He allways called her little girl when he was worried about her, even though she was thirty. She stopped for a half pound of melt away mints at the candy store, her favorites. She bought muffins for the week at the bakery and checked out three historical novel's at the library, also her favorite's. She ran into Clem Weeks in front of her garage and stopped for a chat. Seems strange to see you in civilian clothes. Clem Weeks said, gesturing to the creased navy slacks and matching Careligan blouse Nellie wore. About as strange as I'd looke without my overalls, I guess. Nellie smiled and nodded. It was hard to imagine Clem without her grease streaked overall's and base ball cap. It struck her for a moment that Clem might be cute if she weren't such a grease monkey. But it does make life simple, doesn't it? She said. Not worrying about fashtion, I mean, Clem nodded and slapped a wrench against her palm. Yeah, that's for sure. Nellie could tell that Clem was working up the courage to suggest they get together sometime and wondered how she could avoid it. Granted, they had plenty in common Clem's childhood had been as tough as Nellie's and they both hid behind their work and their shyness. She knew Clem must be hungry for a friend intown that still remembered the details of her unhappy upbringing. But Nellie couldn't imagine being that friend at all. Besides, what in the world they talk about? Carbunators and car diograms? Then again, it might be nice to have a friend who understood her, someone different from mom. Mom drew her out, but sometime her inability to understand how Nellie felt about things frustrated Nellie. With that thought in mind, she latched onto the first idea that came to her. Say Clem, I was wondering. I know you're busy, but...She hesitated. Clem looked hopeful. Nellie plunged ahead. About a car. I don't have one. And I was thinking maybe I should. Clem's eyes brightened, Sure. That's a swell idea, Nellie, but I don't know much about car's. And I was thinking, maybe you could look around for me. I mean, I'm not in any hurry. The truth was, she'd never had the least interest in a car. But maybe it would smooth the way, give them something to talk about for a while. But if you ran across something, well, you could let me know. Clem fidgeted woth her wrench. Yeah, I could do that. So they talked a few more minutes, and when Nellie walked away, she didn't feel so guility. Or quite so alone. So the next Saturday Nellie cooked dinner for Bobby, to calebrate their ingagement. They had a good time and in a few weeks they were married. In the Pine Bluff Court House in the year of 2000, the door bell rang it was Nellie's younger brother Floyd, his wife Laura passed away two years ago, and he was still greving over the lost of his son, Floyd Jr Floyd's wife had not been dead a whole year. Before her oldest son Cedric passed away. Floyd has been drinking heavy. Because he had lost his whole family in a very short period of time. It was very hard on him. and he is still in bad shape. About his family. And when Floyd would come over to Bobby and Nellie's house they would try to cheer him up with a few drinks and just talk about it. There was two woman trying to get with him, but the pain was so strong until he could not pick one to settle down with.. Until later on about three year's after his wife's death. He told Nellie that he thought that he had fallen in love with one of the ladys, but they would argue. All the time, and she didn't like his friend's because she felt that the, well most of the friends wasn't really friend's. One while I think that she was cooking and cleaning up his house and trying to spend more time with him. But she thought that his friends would allways get their way. Floyd would go to their gatherings and leave her out. They still see each other and talk on the phone. Saying things they shoulden say, makeing each other mad and jelous. Just pushing them botton's that nobody else can. I think that's very hurtful and dangerous. But you know everyone relationships are not clean, peceful, settle and tradional. So maybe they are surriveing the only way that they can. But most therapist or psychologist. And me would say maybe that's not the norm. And they should seek some professional therapy. I am sure things might get better for them. The last time Nellie talked to Floyd. He seemed a lot better. Nellie has stoped worrying abot Floyd because he really sound real and happy. Bobby had to go to the store while Nellie was cooking dinner. She remembered her doctor. The main one is doctor Dharamsey at the cancer and Cardiac Center in Pine Bluff. This man, and his staff has been so important in Nellie's and Bobby life. Because they kept most of her appontments, for all most twenty years now. Dharamsey and his has been so percise, loving, down to earth and attentive to Nellie and her heart condition. Until she is so thankful that god refered her to these people to help with her condition. This doctor has been the only one that found out just what was wrong with her. And started to treat it it with every thing he knew. To save her life and help her to live a while longer. The rest of the staff is very intentive also. The nurses, and two special people name Clyde, and Randy. They helped her, and became like friend's. Thaey talked, argued and got pised off at each other, specially Randy. But they can still talk and remain friends. Her doctor Dehramsey seem like a brother of her's. He even said that Nellie remind him of his mother. And doctor Dehramsey is is the best heart doctor in Arkansas right here in Pine Bluff. The doctor treat her condition like he does all of his patients, with compassion, and understanding your fear. He made her focus on God by saying we are by the grace of god, we will teeat this and we will get those this by the grace of god. This blowed her mine because she hadn't ever heard a doctor say those words before. And this manna of specking made Nellie feel more sucure and in good hands. And we need more of this bedside manna. Especially now durring this time of the corona virus. She thought how hard Bobby use to work when he first started working on the grounds of JRMC Hospital. He worked hard, she usc to take him lunch all most everyday. His body in continaous motion, his movement's methodical but fluid. After the first hour he took off his sweat drenched shirt and she could see that he was all lean sinew. His back and chest and arm's were dark brown, despite the fact the summer was long gone. His hair was dark with some gray because it was in his gen's to get gray young in life on he's father's side. It was filled with perspiration, his torso slick with it. But he never slowed down, never paused to res. When she realized there was something in her that admired the way he worked and the picture he made while she was watching and waiting with his lunch from the car. His T shirt was streaked with dirt and perspiration. His hair was slicked back, also damp, his face ruddy from exertion. His arm's seemed to have swelled with his efforts. Nellie felt as if a flock of hummingbird's had been unleashed high in her chest. Light headedness overtook her. She tightened her grip on the car door. He nodded. Thanks for lunch Thanks? She felt the tension she'd been carrying in her neck and shoulder's ever since he'd arrived, it didn't dissipate. She was worn out. And she still had to run to the drug store. The person who continued to surprise Bobby the most and give him the most hope was Nellie. Oh, lord, he was wading into deep water here. BJ and Jarome means a lot to me, she said. I...You know, not having any kid's of my own alive and not...Well, anyway... From the tone of her voice, it sounded as if she thought of herself as an old maid. She must be all of thirty, and so fresh faced, so young herself. She bit her lowerlip and looked down. He realized he'd been staring, had made her nervous. Hey like you, Bobby said. A lot. I'm glad." Are you? He started to reply, but realized his throut was tight now, too. His whole body was pounding woth some kind of expectation. He simply nodded. He had to get out of here. If he didn't, he was going to do something he would regret. Something ...He might kiss her. Startled by the sudden awareness, he backed away, bumping into a kitchen chair. It scraped across the flood, teetered. He grabbed it and righted it and took another step backward in the direction of the door. Calling BJ and Jarome! His voice came out tinged with desperation. Make it snappy! We've got to get you home. His finger's ached to touch her, to feel skin that must be softer than anything he could imagine. Panic welled up. What was happening to him? He started to yell for his son's again when BJ and Jarome reappeared. Okay, okay, BJ said, handing the red and blue costume to Nellie. I'm ready. Bobby put a hand on his son's narrow shoulder and pointed him toward the door. Will I see you tomorrow? It was Nellie, close behind them, her voice as soft as a whisper in his ear. He couldn't catch a full breath. He had to remind himself that she wasn't talking to him. She was talking to his son. He hurried out the door. The cool early evening air helped clear his head. Nellie was not a woman he could want to kiss. Nellie was kind to his son's but she damn sure had no reason to be kind to him. If she ever had a hint what he'd been thinking, she'd call her mama and they'd bring out the tar and feathers. Wanting to kiss Nellie was the worst kind of insanity. If he thought people came down hard ion himnow, he could just imagine what kind of hell would break loose if he laid ahand on the towns very own Florence Nightingale. Nellie felt unsettled. She liked her life in perfect order. Nothing in her world out of place, everything secure under her gentle control. Thing's felt safe that way. On the surface thing's still looked pretty orderly. Nellie still rose every morning at six thirty, ate her own lunch at eleven fortyfive, go out on Saturday or just took that afternoon off. The mail still came on time each day, and the paycheck's from Mrs. E'S estate arrived like clock work. An older sick lady she worked and took care of. But there were hicher in the plan, hesitation's in the second hand of Nellie's inner clock. There was Bobby and there was BJ and Jarame, and mostly there was what was happening in Nellie's head and heart. None of that was under her control, and sometime's that made her breath run shallow and her heart pump from someplace deep within. Someplace she wasn't accustomed to going. She didn't trust what was happening to her. The smell of baking cookie's filled the house. Oatmeal and spices and raisins. She checked the clock oven the refrigerator. Two minutes. Maybe she would peek. As she reached for the pot holder, the back screen door creaked. That would be Bobby. She wasn't even afraid anymore, she realized. She trusted the man he seemed to have become. But she didn't trust herself, or her reaction to him. She turned away from the oven toward the noisy screen door. She turned and watched as he came in. He wore jeans and an old gray sweatshirt, frayed at the ribbed cuffs and collar. His boot's were scuffed. All of Bobby, she realized, looked a little battered, even his dark guarded eye's. Seeing him like this still set her heart beating at a different pace. If it wasn't fear, then what? He still spoke little enough, and Nellie realized she sometime's said thing's in hope's of getting a response from him. His voice seemed to curl up somewhere inside her, brushing against her like a kitten, appealing in it's softness. She bit her lip. I saw the recipe on the back of the oatmeal box she said. I thought I'd try it. See how close it comes to the real thing. Smell's close to me. He almost grinned. Brought me all the way in from the she'd. Nellie smiled, continued studying him. Why did he draw her so? Then she remembered the cookie's and glanced up at the clock with a little gasp. It's time." She took the cookies sheet out and turned off the oven. Bobby walked over and studied the oblong pan of golden brown cookies. They have to cool first, she said. He was close. She surprised herself, sometime, that they could have touched if that had ever been on there minds.

Close enough that sometimes their shoulder's brushed or her hand grazed his arm. Close enough that she knew he smelled of the outdoors fresh air and burning leaves and newly turned soil. The smell of a man. Her mouth went dry. She backed away. He was looking at her oddly, she thought. Those eye's of his coming out of his own private hell just long enough to look into her's. She couldn't seem to turn away just stood there captured by his searching gaze. His mouth was set in the hard lines she'd grown so familiar with. His hair was wind blown. Brought another reaction lurching to the surface of Nellie's consciousness. A spark. A jolt. A wave. Of desire. I'm not real good at this father business. Not much practice." She thought again of touching him, a comforting hand on his shoulder. A way to sympathizer. What was happening to her? It takes time. He's not used to you yet. He got used to you in a hurry. She shrugged. I'm a woman. Like the kid's mother. That was all she'd meant. Wasn't it? But she realized even as she rationalized that she'd been hoping to make Bobby notice. I know, he said. When he looked at her again, his eyes weren't riveted on hers. Instead, they made a slow intimate study of her face. She told herself she should move, look away, do something to break the spell. But she couldn't. She simply stood there, accepting the gaze that was as real as a touch and feeling herself go soft and weak. She felt a sigh rising to her lips. A sigh that deemed like an admission of surrender. Let's...ah...The cookies. They're probably cool enough. After a moment he nodded. But he appeared to move only under protest, just like Nellie. She'd heard about women who came under the spell of men with evil intent and wondered if this was what it was like. Ridiculous, she told herself as she began to lift the cookies off the baking sheet. Her fingers trembled. Bobby isn't a man with evil intent. Of course a woman falling under that kind of spell would think precisely that. She and Bobby and his son's ate oatmeal cookies and drank milk at the kitchen table. She studied Bobby closely, looking for the telltale signs that marked him as evil. She didn't see any, but that could hardly be called conclusive evidence. She watched him closely after that, labeling her feelings for him dangerous even as those feelings began to spiral out of control. One afternoon she watched him waylay BJ and Jarome as the boys darted into the yard after school. BJ brushed him off, beating his father back with unyieulingly petulant look children master so easily. Jarome came in and lavished his need for attention on Nellie. Another afternoon she watched as he discovered an injured squirrel in the yard.

She almost turned away assuming he would put it out of it's misery and unwilling to witness the violence that would nevertheless be an act of mercy. He pulled on his work gloves, brought a box from the shed filled with clean rag's. Then gently he picked up the squirrel, placed it on the bed of rag's and got into his truck. It was two days before she ran into the town vet on the street and learned that Bobby had taken the injured squirrel into be treated. The squirrel would be ready to be released soon, the spell around her heart grew stronger everyday. While she was at her mothers house she had untied her robe to change back into street clothes when she saw the man stride up the street. He caught her eye and she paused. Even before he passed beneath the halo of the streetlight, she knew from the regid angle of his shoulders that it was Bobby and that he was coming for her. She wasn't suree why he'd be coming for her, but she knew it was so. Sticking her head into her moms room, she whispered, it's only Bobby. Don't worry. The comment struck her as odd, all things considered. Her own lack of concern as she opened the door for him also struck her as strange. But she knew the truth of what she felt. It was Bobby. It was nothing to worry about. What's wrong? She asked gently. His face shifted and softened as he looked at her. Nellie realizes he was struggling to hang on to what ever fierce emotions had driven him here. But it was too late. Looked defeated and weary, confused by his presence at her door. She reached out, took him by the arma and led him into the house. Want coffee? He nodded and followed her to the kitchen. She turned on the light and in minutes had a pot of coffee breiving. He stood beside the table, staring at the floor. In the bright kitchen light, the circles beneath his eye's were pronounced, testimony to the fact that the things troubling Bobby were thing's of long standing. A good night's sleep, Nellie suspected, was arare commodity for him. She urged him to sit, then took out cups and milk and spoons. His shoulders sagged, the way they had the day is the kid's okay? He nodded. His voice was barely audible. Nellie wondered at that. The coffee maker gurgled to a stop and she filled two cup's. She doctored Bobby's the way he liked it, with a touch of milk and plenty of sugar. She sipped at hers, black. What's wrong, Bobby? She asked again. He nersed his coffee for a long time, stirring, sipping, into it for answers. She waited. He think's I will hurt you. She sighed. Why on earth ...? Who would have said such a thing? My cousin. Paul. He came to the house. Told me to leave you alone. Bobby's face twisted bitterly. She covered his free hand with her's. Before she realized what she was doing. We'll both talk to him we'll explain. He He studied her, then pulled his hand back. Explain what, Nellie? Well, that you wouldn't hurt me." Wouldn't I? The edge was in his voice again. Nellie sat back in her chair, inching away from him of course not. I wish thing's weren't so tangled up, she said.

His anger ebbed. So do I. I'll make it right with Paul. He shook his head. It's my problem. You're not the only one who cares Bobby. Nellie hurt with him. She could hear the anguish in every word. She had nothing but compassion for Bobby. No more anger, no more blame, certainly no more fear. How could she be thinking these things? Looking at his somber face, at his tortured eye's, how could she not? She touched him again. He gripped her hand. His flesh scraped against hers, heated and hard. She began to tingle with the contact. She groped for something to say, some way to break the spell of this connection and her reaction. She saw the injured pride flicker in his eye's. She wanted to ease what she saw there, but didn't know how. Oh, Bobby...She leaned close. To kiss him on the cheek, but that was a lie and it took only a split second for her to realize the truth. She pressed her lips to his, they were hard, full, his breath hot. Her head began to spin as a tempest of yearning and desire whirled up inside her. Don't do that, Nellie. Ever. His voice was gruff, a low growl of a warnming. She felt her body spring to life as if she'd just been hooked into a source of power. She brushed her lip's over his, willing his to solften and accept her. He grabbed her then, pulling her to him, covering her lip's with his. A hard, hot, brief kiss. Something in her expanded and exploded. It was over too quickly. He thrust her away and glared at her, a look she knew intimately after all these week's. It made her smile.

I'm going. You'll come back, she said. You don't know what you're doing. That much was true. He stalked out, almost ran out, as if he were afraid of what had happened between them. Nellie wasn't afraid. She's still didn't understand why this was happening. She had to be crazy. But she wasn't afraid. She had been all her life, it sometimes seemed. But not any longer. She went after him, hoping to catch him and make him understand how things were changing. But when she reached the front porch, Clem watched him hurry away, then glanced back at Nellie. Nellie caught the lapels of her robe and clutched them to her throat. She knew her face was red, and she could still feel his kiss like a vivid brand on her lips. Clem walked up the step's. You okay? Nellie nodded. She needed to explain. But how? You want to look at this car? Not... not tonight, Clem. I'm sorry. It's okay. Tomorrow's soon enough. She jingled the keys in the pocket of her overall's. I guess I feel sorry for him. You do? Clem gave her a faint smile. I know what it's like. Feelig you don't fit in, that people are alway's talking about you. Nellie saw the forlorn look flicker across Clem's girlish face. She was lonely, too. Nellie remembered all the talk about Clem's mother, the reputation that must have haunted Clem her whole life. And Nellie hadn't been able to reach out in friendship before because of the thing's that haunted her. She realized Clem couldn't know that Nellie's aloofness had nothing to do with the young mechanic's family baggage. Peeople don't talk you, Clem, she said softly. Sure they do. She smiled again. Anyway, I think I understand how he feels. You do, too, don't you? No, I...Nellie felt the heat rising in her face again. It's his son's I worry about. We misfits have to stick together. Nellie wanted to deny it, but it was true. She was a lot like Clem, retreating from the mainstream of life in Pine Bluff so people wouldn't see her emotional scars. Bobby's return was forcing her out of her hiding place. She returned Clem's smile. I have fresh coffee. You could tell me about the car. Yeah? From the tone of her voice, Clem couldn't believe she was being unvited in. Yeah. Bobby spent the next few days trembling inside. For a drink. He felt as bad as he had at eighteen, sitting in the city jail cell, wondering how he could be in the fix hanging out on the corner in Chicago with a gang of friend's, and one of his friend's were guilty of a unbelievable crime. Because the rest of the guys and Bobby was close and they could not believe that they didn't see this kind of evil in this one name been. Did to girl the y all knew was off limit's. Because of her age. In Bobby's mine he felt charged woth anxiety, he took his oldest son to school and picked him up. They talked little. He'd given up trying to explain to BJ that he hadn't hurt anybody just because he knew the fellow that did. Because Nellie was naive and gentle and touched a place in his heart he'd kept sealed away from the rest of the world for years. He finnally could be himself. He thought about her when he gassed up the truck, the bewilderment in her brown eye's, the soft, searching curiosity of her kiss. My god, she'd kissed him! How could he have let that happen? His finger's fumbled with the gas cap when he tried to replace it on his truck. Cold sweat, colder than the spiting rain, dampened his t shirt. When someone called his name, he jumped guiltily and dropped the gas cap. He turned toward the voice. A vaguely familiar looking man stood on the other side of the gas pump's besides a big shiny Sedan. The man thrust his hand between the pump's his smile struck Bobby as determined to prove a lack of prejudice. Terry Washinton Bobby." He remembered now. Washinton had been in his graduating class. Valedictorian or student body president or something. Maybe both. Terry Washinton hadn't given Bobby the time of day back then. Cock sure and spotless, he was for too good for the likes of Bobby Addison. Bobby nodded and took his hand. Terry still looked spotless, from his razor cut hair that had never been touched by fudgie to the black Sedan that said he'd lived up to every ounce of his youthful potential. How's it going, being back home? Terry asked as Bobby retrieved the gas cap that had rolled under his pickup. Pretty good, Bobby said if you don't count the fact that Hud's hardware sold out of dead bolt's the day after I rolled into town. Terry finished pumping his own gas and walked with Bobby, to the cashier. Heard you're workig for Dennis Grant. You worked in landscaping before you came back if I'm not mistaken. The inquiries were general, Bobby tried not to bristle at the implication he'd been talked about plenty, his entire life rehashed at dinner table's all over town. That's right. Terry peeled off a twenty dollar bill, passed it through the window to the cashier and shook his head. Too bad. Sounds like you're exactly whom I need. Oh? Small talk when he heard it. I'm head master at the blue ridge academy. And we sure do need a ground keeper." Bobby remembered the Blue Ridge Academy for girl's. A private prep school for blue bloods the prevassar crowd. His cousen Paul taught there another reason Bobby couldn't imagine fitting in. And he doubted that the Blue Ridge parents would look favorably on having him hanging around. He paid, Terry had waited. They walked back to their vehicles together. Don't suppose you'd consider making??? Terry said. Pays good at the academy, Terry said. Bobby hesitated. That would simplify every thing. The academy was out of town a few miles. Out of sight out of mind. He would be out of sight of the towns people. And Nellie would be out of his sight. It made sense. It might even give him a chance to see Paul, to figure out a way to mend fence's with his angry cousin. But...I don't imagine my background would stand up to much scrutiny, he said finally, reluctantly. Terry put a hand on Bobby's shouder. Listen, Bobby you've had a tough break in life. No reason that ought to haunt you forever. You let me worry about your background. Terry's support lightened the load on Bobby's shoulder's. It still surprised him how often people in Pine Bluff expressed that kind of belief in him. Even Nellie. Her lips had been so soft. So trusting. He had to do something. Fast. He felt her tugging on him right now. Touching her hair with his big rough hands. Touching her life with his, spoiling her's in the process. If you're sure...Terry beamed. When can you start? Nellie hadn't seen Bobby for almost a week. It felt like a lifetime. She hadn't seen the kids either, and that left an empty place in her day in her heart too. Even her mama seemed listless and cranky, as if she were expecting something that never happened. Nellie told herself that was her imagination. She didn't know what she had expected to happen after she and Bobby kissed, but it wasn't this. Abandonment. It stung. It became a tender ache in her heart. She'd been abandoned before, when her old boy friend left for Detroit Michigan. When she thought about it happening again, it was all she could do to catch her breath. The night of a houling, driving rainstrom, when she found herself without power, she did what she'd told herself all week she wouldn't do. She picked up the phone and dialed his number. His voice had the ability to touch her even over the telephone line. Bobby...I...The power went out. There was a silence. She could almost sense the rhythm of his breathing. She could see the way his frown would deepen, the shadow's descend

over his eye's. The electric company will come soon. But...
Of course, he was right. I think moma is afraid. I don't
work for Dennis Liz husband anymore. So he had
abandoned her. She felt as if the ground had been snatched
out from under her. Oh. Still...I can't come, Nellie. She
hated herself for feeling so weak and needy, and for her
willingness to let him see it. Why not? There was a long
silence. She thought of hangin up, saving him the
embarrassment of finding an answer. Nellie closed her
eyes. She thought of a million way's to pled with Bobby,
and none of them seemed fair. It was too complicated. It
would hurt them both. She was crazy to think otherwise.
She hung up, feeling the ragged rhythm of her heartbeat.
He was right. But it didn't help. So Bobby got together
and took that job and did very well. Nellie and Bobby got
together after that time away from each other. The house
alarm was ringing. It was Bobby comeing back from the
store and he and Nellie watched a movie on tv, while they
enjoyed eating their pop corn then they went to bed. But
Nellie couldn't sleep so she got up and fixed herself a ham
and cheese sandwich, turned the tv on and watched a
movie called Gunfighters Moon. She begain to remember
how her neice Ethel left Memphis and went back home
to Pine Bluff Ark. How she inrolled in school and studied
nurseing and became a lpn. She was so proud of her and
her sister Annette finished a nurseing school after she
stayed in New York for about eight or ten years. She came

back to Arkansas and then persuced this career. How Robert's son Rodney left home got married, had two girls went to nurseing and cheif school. And Liz two girl's win Charleet and Charletta went to nurseing assistant and finished. And Liz youngest girl Caroline was a manager at the little store. She had worked their for a long time before I knew it, because Nellie use to visit her relatives in Chicago, and California. Liz their mother worked for area agency, a while before she took sick with cancer, and lost her battal in 2013. Her death was devastating to Nellie because she spoiled her and the whole family, she was a mothering type of person." Bobby has three children a daughter name Shalona. Shalona lives in Little Rock Arkansas. She was a mother of a little cute boy name Kelaton who is deceased. He drawned in a swimming pool in a park in Little Rock, which was devastating and she is still going through all the stuff you feel when loseing someone so dear to you. Nellie pray for her and all of the love one's. Bobby has a son name Bobby Jr. He's the pround father of a son that's fifteen year's old, name Christifur. And a two year old little girl name Skylar and Bobby has a son name Jarome and he's married and have a son name Blake, ten or eleven year's old and a little girl name Riley and they live in Texas. They are all doing fine under the circumstan. Praise God.

The End

ABOUT THE AUTHOR

Nellie Addison is a certified Cosmetologist and color analyst. She is also a certified nusing assistant. Other than writing, Nellie enjoys cooking, reading, and dancing and traveling.

She loves sharing her stories with all who will listen, and she looks forward to sharing her many other stories.

She currently resides in Pine Bluff, Arkansas.

When you read her books you can identify with some of the sotries and her stories can even help with some of today's problems.

Printed in the United States
by Baker & Taylor Publisher Services